The Bird-Friendly Backyard™

Your Guide to
Food and Feeders

The Bird-Friendly Backyard™

Your Guide to
Food and Feeders

SIMPLE WAYS TO PROVIDE A BOUNTIFUL FEAST

SALLY ROTH

RODALE

WE **INSPIRE** AND **ENABLE** PEOPLE TO IMPROVE
THEIR LIVES AND THE WORLD AROUND THEM

We're always happy to hear from you. For questions or comments concerning the editorial content of this book, please write to:

Rodale Book Readers' Service
33 East Minor Street
Emmaus, PA 18098

Look for other Rodale books wherever books are sold. Or call us at (800) 848-4735.

For more information about Rodale Organic Living magazines and books, visit us at
www.organicgardening.com

On the cover: A female cardinal is just one of the many birds that will visit your yard when you provide the right combination of food and feeders.

Editor: Christine Bucks
Cover and Interior Book Designer: Nancy Smola Biltcliff
Cover and Interior Illustrator: Michael Gellatly
Layout Designer: Faith Hague
Copy Editors: Barbara M. Webb, Sarah S. Dunn
Product Specialist: Brenda Miller
Indexer: Nanette Bendyna

Rodale Organic Living Books

Executive Creative Director: Christin Gangi
Executive Editor: Margot Schupf
Art Director: Patricia Field
Content Assembly Manager: Robert V. Anderson Jr.
Copy Manager: Nancy N. Bailey
Editorial Assistant: Sara Sellar

Library of Congress Cataloging-in-Publication Data

Roth, Sally.
    The bird-friendly backyard : your guide to food and feeders : simple ways to provide a bountiful feast / by Sally Roth.
        p.   cm.
    Includes bibliographical references (p.   ).
    ISBN 0–87596–890–2   (hardcover : alk. paper)
    1. Birds—Feeding and feeds.   2. Gardening to attract birds.   I. Title.
QL676.5 .R6686   2002
598'.07'234—dc21   2002012100

Distributed in the book trade by St. Martin's Press

2   4   6   8   10   9   7   5   3   1   hardcover

Rodale
Organic Gardening Starts Here!

HERE at Rodale, we've been gardening organically for more than 60 years—ever since my grandfather J. I. Rodale learned about composting and decided that healthy living starts with healthy soil. In 1940 J. I. started the Rodale Organic Farm to test his theories, and today the nonprofit Rodale Institute Experimental Farm is still at the forefront of organic gardening and farming research. In 1942 J. I. founded *Organic Gardening* magazine to share his discoveries with gardeners everywhere. His son, my father, Robert Rodale, headed *Organic Gardening* until 1990, and today a third generation of Rodales is growing up with the magazine. Over the years we've shown millions of readers how to grow bountiful crops and beautiful flowers using nature's own techniques.

In this book, you'll find the latest organic methods and the best gardening advice. We know—because all our authors and editors are passionate about gardening! We feel strongly that our gardens should be safe for our children, pets, and the birds and butterflies that add beauty and delight to our lives and landscapes. Our gardens should provide us with fresh, flavorful vegetables, delightful herbs, and gorgeous flowers. And they should be a pleasure to work in as well as to view.

Sharing the secrets of safe, successful gardening is why we publish books. So come visit us at www.organicgardening.com, where you can tour the world of organic gardening all day, every day. And use this book to create your best garden ever.

Happy gardening!

Maria Rodale

Maria Rodale
Rodale Organic Living Books

Contents

Beyond Sunflower Seeds

*The secret to attracting birds is no secret at all:
Offer food and they will come.*

WHAT'S the draw of even bothering to feed birds at all, you ask? Well, the reasons for feeding birds are as plentiful as the crowds at your feeders. A yard full of birds means a healthier garden because, no matter how well stocked the feeder, birds still eat zillions of bugs. It also means a more interesting scene, with song and motion and color adding life to the back-

yard. Watching birds is great therapy for stress or boredom—as well as just plain fun.

Your helping hand can make life easier for birds by giving them a reliable source of nourishing food. And sometimes, feeders can even make a life-or-death difference—something I learned firsthand.

Snow is a rarity in our little corner of southern Indiana, which I'll use as my excuse for getting caught unprepared when a blizzard came sneaking in a few winters ago. The storm started innocently enough in late afternoon, just a light dusting of snow flurries that brought more than the usual number of customers to the feeders. Crowds of juncos and white-throated sparrows scratched about on the ground below trays crowded with cardinals, the single towhee had multiplied to six, blue jays cracked seeds without squabbling, and every block of suet had a waiting line of woodpeckers.

I was thrilled at the abundance of birds, and I poured out seed with abandon, keeping the feeders brimming until dark settled in. Next morning, I was awakened by my young son's cry of delight.

"Look at all the snow!" he hollered.

Opening a sleepy eye, I peered out the window beside the bed and saw nothing but white. The yard looked like a foreign landscape, with familiar landmarks disguised under mounds and drifts of the white stuff.

"It's a blizzard!" I hollered right back, grabbing for sweatpants and slippers and hurrying to open the door and get a look outside.

It was definitely a blizzard—2 feet of fresh, beautiful snow.

"No school!" yelled my son.

No birdseed, thought I.

All my generosity the day before, when the boost in bird customers should have alerted me a storm was coming, had pretty much emptied the 50-pound sack of sunflower seed. Even the big metal can of millet was down to scrapings. Any uneaten seed was buried deep, but as my eyes adjusted to the glare, I saw that despite the early hour, birds were already at work, trying to excavate their now-vital breakfast.

A determined cardinal had managed to scratch down to seed level in one roofed feeder, while a bunch of clever goldfinches had made themselves at home right on the front porch, where seed spilled in the scooping was buried by only a shallow drift. A band of chickadees and tufted titmice swung in the trees, chattering what sounded like encouragement while they sought any overwintering insects they might have missed on earlier forays. Even a crow, which I'd never seen alight in the yard before, skulked on a tree limb, waiting to see what would turn up.

I've always thought that feeding birds is a much better deal for the host than for the birds. All they get is a meal, while we get hours of entertainment, a lively presence in the backyard, extra protection for our garden plants, and a lifetime of learning and pleasure. Now it was time for payback. The birds in my backyard needed my help to stay alive.

Luckily, though the birdseed supply was all but gone, my kitchen was well stocked. In no time, we had feeders swept, exposing any leftovers from the day before. While the birds flocked to that seed, we set about putting ingenuity to work. For our insect-eating friends, the woodpeckers, robins, and bluebirds, we soaked protein-rich dry dog food in water to soften it and mixed up a big batch of peanut butter/cornmeal dough, stretching it even further with some stale breakfast cereal.

For the seed-loving sparrows, juncos, and finches, I sacrificed my big bouquet of dried foxtail grass to the cause, laying the sheaf of seedheads right on the ground, where they were eagerly adopted. Unpopped popcorn was a big hit with the cardinals.

We chopped blocks of suet from the freezer into bite-size nibbles for the eat-anything birds like blue jays and starlings but soon found every bird wanted a hearty sample of the stuff—especially the bluebird family, who settled themselves on the backs of the porch rocking chairs, waiting to see what was next on the menu.

By the end of the day I'd recycled every box of stale cereal, every scrap of bread, every slice of lunch meat, and almost 40 pounds of dog food. Plus a couple of economy-size jars of peanut butter, the pecans and black walnuts I'd collected for Christmas baking, every child-size box of raisins, and every last grape rolling around in the fruit bin.

I was tired. But the birds were well fed—and satisfied.

I like having a good supply of favorite seeds and special treats for all my backyard birds. But I also like knowing that if I get caught short on birdseed, my birds won't go hungry.

As you learn who eats what and why, you'll discover that feeding birds doesn't end with a sack of sunflower seed. That's only the beginning.

1
BIRD FEEDING 101

WHO BENEFITS THE MOST from feeding wild birds—the birds or us? We probably get the best end of the deal. After all, feeding backyard birds allows us to feel connected with wild creatures that otherwise wouldn't notice us, and we get the daily wonders of a yard filled with a wide variety of feathered friends.

Feeder Birds

CERTAIN birds are so well adapted to taking advantage of bird feeders and so widespread in their range that you can expect to see them just about anywhere. Friendly chickadees, finches, jays, and juncos crop up at feeders from California to Maine. Learning the names of regulars is the easiest way to start bird watching. You'll have the luxury of looking at a bird long enough to find it in a field guide, and you'll have the pleasure of getting to know the personalities and behavior of different species.

The arrival of uncommon visitors is what makes feeding birds so much fun. At migration time in spring, unusual birds may stop over for a bite of fast food before they take to the skies again, or they may visit to restore their energy before settling down nearby. Fall arrivals are more predictable and provide just as much pleasure. In fall, the regular feeder guests grow by several species as northern birds take up residence for the winter.

Winter storms can bring unexpected customers. In inclement weather when natural pickings are unreliable or nonexistent, horned larks or snow buntings may come in from the farm fields, bluebirds may travel long distances from their usual sheltering hedgerows, and birds of prey may patrol or even sample some suet.

WHO WILL COME?

The birds you can expect to host at your feeder will depend on where you live and what your wild surroundings are like. If your property adjoins or is near grasslands, you may get regular visits from dicksissels, meadowlarks, quail, or vesper sparrows. In forested areas of the Northwest, the varied thrush, towhee, and fox sparrow will be regulars. In forested areas of the Midwest, you will never see a varied thrush, but the spectacular scarlet tanager may honor you with its presence.

Seed eaters are the best customers at feeders because the menu is tailored to their natural preferences. Their numbers include scores of interesting species, from grosbeaks and goldfinches to the curious crossbills and sparrows. Woodpeckers are fond of feeders, too, and will certainly eat their fill.

Many insect-eating birds, including flycatchers, robins, wood warblers, wrens, and others, also enjoy berries and soft foods such as suet, which may lure them to your feeding station, especially when hunger is strong and natural food is scarce. Don't expect to see strictly insectivorous birds at your feeder, however: Swallows and swifts, for instance, will not be interested in your offerings. No matter how delectable, feeder food just can't compete with insects on the wing.

Common Visitors

WITH a few regional variations, the following birds are most likely to visit your backyard feeders:

Cardinals	House sparrows	Starlings
Chickadees	Jays	Titmice
Doves	Juncos	Woodpeckers
Finches, such as goldfinches and house finches	Native sparrows, such as song sparrows and tree sparrows	
	Nuthatches	

Bird Feeding 101

Q This spring was the first time I'd put up hummingbird feeders, and I was delighted with quite a show. Can I keep the feeders up all year? I'm concerned that if I do, I'll be encouraging the hummingbirds to stay around instead of migrate. What do you think?

A No need to worry: Birds migrate according to an internal timetable set to the hours of daylight, not because your food is too good to leave behind. Keep your nectar feeder up: After the bulk of hummingbirds depart, it can be a lifesaver for stragglers.

Q My neighbor swears red pepper keeps squirrels from eating birdseed, but I have my doubts. Is she right?

A Your neighbor is definitely on to something. Birds aren't affected like mammals by the irritating capsaicin in hot peppers. Spraying your seed with pepper extract or buying treated seed will discourage squirrels strongly. In winter, when food is scarce, give squirrels their own feeder of untreated seeds, corn, and nuts, or they may overcome their aversion and eat the hot stuff anyway. (See "Treated Seed" on page 28 for more information about red pepper and birdseed.)

Q I have a lot of feeders set up in my backyard and love watching the many different types of birds that come to visit. But I've often wondered whether I'm doing more harm than good. Can feeding birds can change their natural habits?

A That's a good question—with no solid answer. No one knows for certain how big a part backyard feeders play in the expanding and changing ranges of American birds because other factors such as habitat loss, climate changes, and temporary weather conditions also play a part.

Avian Education

LEARNING about the basic foods and the treats that bring wild birds flocking is an education all by itself. Knowing what to feed will help you fine-tune the offerings at your feeders so that the guests you can expect will be provided for with little waste. And knowing when to feed is vital for the birds who will quickly become regulars at your feeding station. Birds go to their accustomed places to find food first—if the cupboard is bare, they will soon head off to seek sustenance someplace else.

EVERY BEAK TELLS A STORY

Birds fall into three main categories: seed eaters, insect eaters, and berry eaters. If you want a backyard filled with a variety of birds, you need to offer a menu that's pleasing to a host of avian palates. In addition, you need to figure out where birds like to dine, so you can place their food where they're most likely to find it.

You can find out what different birds like to eat by taking a look at their beaks (also known as bills). Depending on the size, shape, and strength of their beaks, birds can shell sunflower seeds, chisel into wood after a grub, or snap tiny gnats out of the air. For example, sparrows, buntings, and other birds that eat small seeds have small beaks. Birds that seek out large seeds of maples, spruces, and pines, such as grosbeaks and cardinals, have bigger, more powerful beaks than other seed-eating birds. Swallows and swifts, which eat

Cardinals use their powerful beaks to eat large seeds, such as these from pine trees.

only insects, have puny beaks, while fish eaters, like herons, have long pointed bills. (For more on birds and beaks, see "A Guide to Beaks and Bills" on this page.)

WHERE BIRDS EAT

Now that you know what birds like to eat, turn your attention to where they like to dine. Think of your yard as a three-story café.

The top floor is trees. It's for birds of the treetops, who spend most of their life in the leafy canopy over your head. Their nests are usually high in trees, and they're usually insect eaters, filling their bellies with the caterpillars and insects they glean from the foliage. Tanagers, orioles, vireos, warblers, cuckoos, and grosbeaks are top-floor diners.

The middle story of your backyard café is shrubs, tall grasses, and flowers. It's for birds like cardinals, catbirds, thrashers, wrens, sparrows, and some warblers that like cover off the ground.

Your lawn and garden beds—the ground-level area—is the dining

A Guide to Beaks and Bills

PUTTING out the welcome mat for birds is easier if you know what they like to eat. And what they like to eat depends on what kind of beak they have. Here's a quick look at 11 common birds and their beaks.

BIRDS	BEAKS	FOOD PREFERENCES
Finches, sparrows, cardinals	Short, strong-looking, conical	Seeds and nuts
Hawks, owls	Strong, sharply curved	Meat
Hummingbirds	Long, narrow	Flower nectar
Spoonbills, ducks	Wide, flat, spoon-shaped	Small fish and aquatic insects
Vireos, orioles, tanagers	Slim, long	Insects and fruit

spot for birds that prefer to pull worms or grubs, scratch in the leaves for insects, or pick up seeds. Robins and grackles on the lawn are ground level birds in action. So are the blackbirds, thrushes, sparrows, juncos, quail, pheasants, and towhees that you may have noticed hanging out below your feeders, in your meadow garden, or beneath your shrubs.

Your bird-feeding goal is to fill all three stories of your backyard café with treats for the birds. So plant trees—even when the trees are very young, they'll attract the insects that birds enjoy. And it won't be long before those trees are producing nuts and seeds, too.

To make the birds of the brush feel at home, plant a variety of shrubs to re-create a natural hedgerow and let some areas of grass or annual flowers grow thick and undisturbed. Sparrows and other ground feeders will do fine on your lawn, in a meadow garden, or under shrub plantings in a shady garden.

Grackles prefer to do their dining at ground level, so sprinkle some seeds for them at the base of your feeder.

Feeding Stations

THE more feeders you have in your backyard, the greater the variety of birds that will come to visit. When you combine a cluster of diverse feeders, you create what is known as a feeding station: a place where birds of all kinds can come to satisfy their need for food. (For detailed information on specific kinds of feeders, see Chapter 3, "Feeder Fundamentals," on page 65.)

MUST-HAVES

Seed feeders and suet feeders are the basics for any feeding station. They will supply the needs of nearly all birds that commonly visit backyards, from chickadees to jays.

Tray feeders are ideal for feeding a crowd. If you prefer to keep your seed protected and not in a help-yourself buffet, you can create extra feeding room by adding more hopper-style or other enclosed feeders. Tube feeders are another good choice.

Suet feeders are always busy in winter, when this nutritious high-fat food provides ready calories to keep birds warm. Because suet feeders are small, you can provide several at your feeding station to accommodate more customers.

SPECIALIZED FEEDERS

To attract birds that don't depend mainly on seeds, you may decide to include other specialized feeders at your station. Fruit feeders and soft-food feeders that can hold doughnuts and other delights are a good place to start. Supplement these with nut feeders and corn feeders, and your feeding station will be ready to cater to just about any birds on the block.

Make sure to feed birds when they need it. Birds are hungry first thing in the morning. And although they may snack off and on all day long, they come out to eat seriously again in the afternoon, to fuel their bodies for the coming night.

Include several feeding devices on which to offer mockingbirds, orioles, and other fruit eaters their favorite treats. A simple nail-spike feeder is perfect for skewering half an apple or orange. Small open trays are good places to pour a few handfuls of dried or fresh berries and grapes. And a plastic plant saucer makes a fine impromptu fruit feeder since it won't absorb the juice.

To cater to bluebirds, provide a place in your feeding stations to offer mealworms. You'll want a separate feeder for these bluebird favorites, where the shier birds can dine in peace on their favorite treats. Position the bluebird mealworm feeder several yards from feeders frequented by aggressive guests, with an intervening shrub or trellis if possible. Or just let your bluebirds learn to share with other mealworm lovers, such as Carolina wrens.

ADDED ACCESSORIES

For a complete feeding station, make provisions for the other needs of birds. Grit, salt, and water will make your feeding station a one-

---

FEEDING STATIONS
at a glance

IF you want to attract a wide variety of birds, your feeding station should include:

■ A basic feeder, such as a seed feeder

■ A fruit or soft-food feeder

■ Nut and corn feeders

■ A salt block

■ Grit, such as crushed eggshells

■ A water source, such as a birdbath

---

stop shop for any bird. Clear an area for a salt block, protecting the soil beneath it and any nearby plants from leaching by lining the area with heavy-duty plastic. The shallow lid from a large plastic storage container is a good solution;

cover it with a thin layer of wood chips to make it look better. Scatter grit or eggshells on open lawn, over bare soil, or in a low tray feeder.

Coarse sand is an ideal source of grit for birds. Buy the sand at a building supply store, not in the children's play area. Soft, white sandbox sand may be great to play in, but it is too fine for birds. River sand is ideal because of its large grain size. If you have a gravel or river-rock operation nearby, ask if you can buy a few scoops (they'll probably let you have some for free). It's a good idea to keep the supply of grit in the same place year after year so that your birds get accustomed to a reliable source.

Watching birds sip and splash in the bath is just as entertaining as watching them dine. Adding a birdbath or other water source near your feeders will accommodate birds and give you a great place to watch them bathe and drink. Keep the water far enough away from feeders to keep shells and other debris from falling in the bath. If your space is limited, a good solution is to hang a shallow basin from a hook or tree branch near a low, ground-level feeder.

Plants also add to the appeal of a feeding station, making it look more attractive to both you and the birds. Berry bushes, such as blueberries and sumac, along with other plantings that offer fruit or seeds that attract insects, will satisfy the needs of birds for natural food that they can enjoy in every season.

Finally, don't despair if your yard is full of rocks and stones—rocks make terrific bird feeders and watering holes. For feeder purposes, you'll want a rock with a slightly concave surface so that it can hold seed, grit, or even water. Low, wide rocks are ideal because their weight is less than that of tall, wide rocks and also because they look more natural in the landscape. If you must use a high rock, bury at least a third of its height below the soil surface, the way it would be settled in nature. A single smallish rock—less than 2 or 3 feet across—looks forlorn by itself in a garden. If a giant rock is out of the question, group three medium-size rocks together to create a "feeder" of good visual weight. (Also make sure to use a rock that is native to your area so that it doesn't look out of place.)

Bird Feeding 101

Q Although I garden organically, I'm concerned about using BTK (*Bacillus thuringiensis* var. *kurstaki*) on my plants. Can this "safe" organic pesticide harm the birds that visit my yard?

A Although BTK doesn't harm birds, it will kill a wide variety of leaf-eating caterpillars. And that's bad news for birds that might make a meal of those caterpillars (and it can cut down on the number of butterflies you enjoy in your yard, too). When you can, let birds handle caterpillar problems in your yard and garden. If caterpillars descend en masse on your plants, be patient: Chances are that catbirds, orioles, and other fans of these crawly creatures will soon arrive to snatch them up.

Q I'm planning a backyard wedding, but I'm concerned about guests throwing rice after the ceremony. I've heard that if birds eat dry rice, it will swell up in their stomachs and kill them. Is there any truth to this claim?

A No truth at all—in fact, rice is a big part of the diet of bobolinks, which regularly scour rice fields in the South. However, birds will usually ignore rice in favor of other foods—so you may end up with a lot of rice covering your lawn.

Q Lately, I've noticed a hawk flying above my backyard every now and then. Is he after the food I've put out in feeders for the birds—or the birds themselves?

A Unfortunately, it's not the seeds and suet in your feeders that tempt hawks—it's the birds dining at your feeder. You can try to give your feeder birds a fighting chance by offering dense cover close to the feeder for fast getaways. Hemlocks and spruces are perfect; a discarded Christmas tree or a pile of branches and other brush serves well as a temporary measure.

Backyard for the Birds

FEEDERS are only the start when it comes to inviting birds to your landscape. After all, staying alive is the number-one concern of all birds. So in addition to food and water, birds need cover from predators (like the neighbor's cat), safe nesting sites, and places to roost. If you keep those things in mind as you plan your bird-friendly backyard, you'll be rewarded with a landscape brimming with birds—who will return year after year.

OUT OF SIGHT

Keeping out of sight is the *modus operandi* for most birds. Sheltering shrubs and other plants protect them from the gaze and the grasp of cats, hawks, and other hungry bird eaters. Design your yard so that there are only small stretches of open space between plantings so that birds can move throughout your property safely.

Be sure to consider winter cover, too, when you're selecting plants. You'll want to include ever-

Predator Control

YOU can't keep every bird safe from every predator, but you can help to eliminate one major threat—cats. Keep your own feline pets indoors, especially during nesting season, and do your best to discourage strays.

To protect birds from hawks, provide them convenient close shelter at feeding areas and water features, so they can dive into dense bushes for a getaway if needed.

Snakes, raccoons, opossums, and owls may also prey on birds, but there's not much you can do to keep these animals out of your yard. Do, however, protect any bird boxes you put up with antipredator baffles on the posts below them. Those sold to keep squirrels or raccoons out of feeders will do the trick for birdhouses as well. Antipredator door guards on nest boxes are also a plus. These plastic or metal tubes extend outward from the entrance hole, making it impossible for a raccoon's paw to reach the eggs inside.

greens for the valuable shelter their branches offer in the off-season, when deciduous species are bare. Remember to choose first those plants that offer food sources in addition to cover: Hemlocks, pines, and other evergreen conifers will eventually produce a bounty of seed-filled cones—as well as insects—among their needles. Broad-leaved evergreens, such as bayberries (*Myrica* spp.) and Oregon grape hollies (*Mahonia* spp.), are other good choices.

HOME COMFORTS

When birds feel comfortable and protected in your yard, they're more likely to move in to raise a family. The plants you provide for protective cover will also supply birds with many good sites for nesting. Shrubs with dense branches, especially those with thorns or prickles, are eagerly sought as nest sites because their branches deter predators. An overgrown patch of raspberries or other brambles is ideal. Hawthorns (*Crataegus* spp.), with their spiny branches, and hollies (*Ilex* spp.), with their prickly leaves, are other plants with good

NESTING MATERIALS
at a glance

YOU can quickly catch the interest of any birds about to build a nest by supplying much-desired materials. Place these materials in an empty tray feeder or on the bare ground, and see what kind of takers you attract.

■ White feathers, especially the curly breast feathers of chickens, ducks, or geese.

■ 6-inch pieces of white string or yarn

■ Fine twigs, 4 to 6 inches long

■ An old grapevine wreath

■ Long blades of dried grass

■ Combings from your dog

■ Dried moss from old floral arrangements

> **Instead of planting a hedge of forsythia, which has little bird value, try a food-providing hedge of bayberry, blueberries, or sumac.**

nesting potential. A dense tangle of vines, such as sweet autumn clematis (*Clematis terniflora*), may also be used as a nest site.

Robins and phoebes may quickly adopt a horizontal, covered shelf—a simplified, open-walled structure that appeals to these birds—as a nest. Birdhouses themselves are eagerly sought by cavity nesters such as chickadees, woodpeckers, wrens, and even owls, as well as the popular bluebird.

SANCTUARY

A densely planted yard also offers birds safe areas to roost at night or in bad weather. Evergreens are especially welcomed for roosting places. If you are lucky enough to already have a large spruce or other evergreen, watch in late afternoon to see what birds fly into its branches. A single 15-foot-tall eastern red cedar (*Juniperus virginiana*) at the corner of my former Pennsylvania home held catbirds, mockingbirds, robins, brown thrashers, and a horde of house sparrows within its dense, prickly branches at night. At my Indiana home, the same kind of tree shelters more than 50 birds every evening in winter: more than a dozen cardinals, plus robins, fox sparrows, white-crowned sparrows, and the ubiquitous house sparrows. Not all birds seek plants for roosting places. Carolina wrens are apt to wiggle their way into garages, sheds, and other outbuildings. My garage at a former home had a circular opening in one wall where a stovepipe had been removed. In the evening, I watched cardinals, Carolina wrens, chickadees, robins, and titmice enter the hole to roost overnight.

Nest boxes, roosting boxes, and natural cavities in trees are also sought for roosts. On cold winter nights, several birds-of-a-feather may pile into one communal box for warmth.

Bird-Friendly Landscaping

BIRDS don't care how good your landscape design skills are. As long as your yard supplies them with food, water, shelter, and a safe way to move about, they'll happily spend hours there. But a yard with bird appeal should also look good to your eyes. Here are some tips to keep in mind.

■ Vary the topography of a flat yard by adding berms, walls, or sunken areas. The changes in surface height will make your yard more interesting, and it will seem bigger, too. Also vary height by including trellised vines and arbors, which will supply more bird plants in a small amount of space.

■ Plant shrubs and young trees in groups. Three dogwoods or hollies planted together are more visually appealing—and more bird appealing—than isolated specimens.

■ Include broad-needled evergreens for textural contrast, four-season greenery, and bird shelter.

■ Experiment with native plants to supply food, nesting materials, and shelter that birds are familiar with.

■ Install birdhouses with entrance holes custom-sized for your favorite birds. Natural wood boxes will soon mellow to gray, blending in with the background instead of standing out like sore thumbs.

■ Place the feeding station in the most accessible site. It's no fun lugging birdseed through winter snowdrifts.

■ Plant a shady garden in layers as in a natural woodland: tall trees, smaller trees or large shrubs, small shrubs, ferns and wildflowers, groundcovers, leaf mulch. It will offer a more appealing habitat.

■ Tie garden areas together with sheltering shrubs or beds so that birds can move safely through your yard.

■ Let some weeds stand to entice small-seed eaters. Delay cutting back garden plants until later winter so birds can shelter among their stems.

Common visitors Feeding stations Home comforts Sanctuary Beaks and bills

Extending the Neighborhood

MAKING your yard attractive to birds is a great start, but if you really want to bring more—and different—birds to your yard, inspire your neighbors to join you. If the yards surrounding yours include the same kind of welcoming features as yours does, you'll end up with a bigger bird-friendly space.

WIN-WIN SITUATION

Property lines are meaningless to birds—an appealing space is just that. If your appealing bird-safe space flows into a neighbor's, birds will move freely from one place to another. Bigger bird-friendly spaces mean more birds, so both you and your neighbors will benefit. If neighboring yards border a wild area, the extension of plantings may eventually create corridors that birds will use to move back and forth from backyards to the natural areas. That can result in species that you wouldn't otherwise see visiting your feeder or watering hole, such as bobwhites or bluebirds.

Often, just the appealing sight of a well-planted yard alive with birds is all it takes to make your neighbors want to create their own little sanctuary. A couple of chats over the backyard hedge can also encourage a boomlet of bird-friendly planting in a neighborhood. Talk to your neighbors about the pleasures of watching birds: the fun of seeing a robin splash in its bath, the thrill of your first junco of the season. Chances are, once your neighbors see how much pleasure you're getting from feeding the birds, they'll want to take part in the fun.

COMMON FOODS

Satisfying the Palates of Backyard Birds

food

Sunflower seed Niger Millet Flaxseed Berries Grapes Nuts Suet Nectar Bread

SETTING THE TABLE for your avian friends can be a simple affair featuring one or two kinds of seed, or a more elaborate spread—one that offers everything from fruit to nuts and cereal to bread. If you keep your feeders well stocked, you'll be able to enjoy watching backyard birds on a regular basis throughout the year, no matter what's on the menu. Of course, if you put out a wide variety of foods (that is, the more elaborate spread), you'll better your chances of welcoming in all kinds of different types of birds. And that's your opportunity to observe new birds you've never seen before!

Preferred Foods

SUNFLOWER seeds, millet, and other feeder staples are the meat and potatoes of most birds' diets. They'll eat them day in and day out because the offerings are abundant and readily available. But birds also have their preferences—that is, the food they seek out first, whether at your feeder or in the wild.

When acorns and beechnuts ripen, for instance, birds will desert the feeder in favor of these natural foods. The juicy fruits of a mulberry tree (*Morus* spp.) will also di-vert the attention of feeder birds that may have come to your place to pick up raisins or other fruity offerings. Watch the action in your yard and you'll see that your gone-to-seed zinnias or the fuzzy thistles that you overlooked in the garden draw a bigger crowd of finches than even the most expensive tube feeder of niger.

Your birds aren't being disloyal by spurning your offerings and turning to wild foods. They're only doing what comes naturally. Each species has its preferences, and they seek the seeds, nuts, nectar, or fruits of plants that best supply the nourishment they need in the natural world.

PERSONAL TASTES

Many species' preferences are easy to determine—goldfinches prefer niger and sunflower seed over other feeder foods, and woodpeckers seek suet with a side order of sunflower seeds. Birds usually go first to feeder foods that most closely resemble their natural diet. But birds also display regional and individual preferences. The cardinals at your feeder may adore safflower seed, while a few hundred miles away the red birds there are reaching for cracked corn.

It's fun to experiment with new foods at the feeder. Think of lists of preferred foods, like the one on page 20, as the standard menu of your bird café. Then add daily specials. Keep track of how quickly your birds take to the new foods and which birds eat what.

When it comes to a meal, a downy woodpecker's first choice in fare is suet.

Quick Reference   FEEDER FAVORITES

EXPECT your feeder birds to head first for the preferred foods on this list. But birds enjoy occasional variety in their diet, too, and will eagerly eat other foods—particularly when their favorites are lacking, or when a disruptive bird is keeping them away from their favored foods.

BIRDS	MOST PREFERRED FOODS	ALSO HIGHLY ENJOYED
Bluebirds	Mealworms, peanut butter	Suet, berries, bread, raisins, fruit
Cardinals	Sunflower seed	Safflower seed, fruit, millet, bread and baked goods, fruit
Chickadees	Peanuts, nutmeats, peanut butter, suet	Sunflower seed, bread and baked goods
Doves, pigeons	Millet	Cracked corn
Finches	Niger, sunflower seed	Millet, pine nuts, peanuts, suet
Goldfinches	Niger, sunflower seed	Millet, flax, canary seed, suet, birdseed mix, grass seed
Grosbeaks	Sunflower seed	Fruit, suet, millet, safflower seed
Jays	Nutmeats, peanuts	Sunflower seed, suet, corn, bread
Juncos	Millet	Sunflower seed, cracked corn, nutmeats, chopped peanuts
Kinglets	Suet	Bread and baked goods
Mockingbirds	Fruit	Bread and baked goods, suet, sunflower seed, birdseed mix
Nuthatches	Nutmeats, suet, peanut butter	Sunflower seed, corn
Orioles	Nectar, oranges	Grape jelly, fruit, suet, raisins
Pheasants	Cracked corn	Millet
Quail	Cracked corn	Millet
Robins	Mealworms, berries, fruit	Suet, bread, raisins
Native sparrows	Millet	Suet, bread and baked goods, sunflower seed
Tanagers	Fruit, suet	Millet, mealworms, bread
Thrashers	Fruit	Birdseed mix, millet, suet
Titmice	Peanuts, peanut butter, nutmeats	Sunflower seed, suet, bread
Towhees	Millet	Sunflower seed, cracked corn, bread and baked goods
Woodpeckers	Suet	Sunflower seed, nectar, fruit
Wrens	Peanut butter, suet	Bread and baked goods, fruit

Sunflower seed Niger Millet Flaxseed Berries Grapes Nuts Suet Nectar Bread   **food**

Birdseed 101

"BIRDSEED" doesn't describe a single seed. It includes a sampling of many grains and other seeds—from feeder staples like sunflower seed and millet to the wheat, corn, and milo fillers used in inexpensive seed mixes. These days, birdseed suppliers are adding an ever-growing lineup of seed mixes to the shelves. You can find bags of seed just for finches, and bags of heftier seeds designed to bring cardinals and grosbeaks. Armed with some knowledge of which birds prefer what seeds and some information about the seeds themselves, you can become a smarter shopper and spend those big birdseed bucks more wisely. Here's a rundown of the best seeds for backyard bird feeding.

SUNFLOWER SEEDS

If you stocked your feeder with nothing but sunflower seeds, you would be able to satisfy more than 20 different species of feeder birds. All large-beaked seed eaters, including cardinals, grosbeaks, and jays, readily eat sunflower seeds.

These birds, who use their big bills to easily crack the shells to free the meaty morsels inside, relish both black oil and gray-striped sunflower seeds. Chickadees, finches, nuthatches, titmice, and many other smaller-beaked feeder regulars also

CUSTOM-BLENDED BIRDSEED
at a glance

Here's a good general-recipe birdseed mix that appeals to many kinds of birds. Using a coffee can as a measuring cup, combine:

- 10 scoops black oil sunflower seed
- 5 scoops millet
- 3 scoops cracked corn
- 2 scoops safflower seed
- 1 scoop flaxseed
- 1 scoop untreated grass seed

food

head for sunflowers as their staple seed of choice.

Black oil sunflower seed is the more economical option because the smaller seeds go further than the big, plump, gray-striped variety, which has fewer seeds per pound. It also has a higher oil content, so it gives the birds more calories when they eat it. The other advantage to black oil sunflower seed is that smaller birds can crack it readily.

NIGER

Niger is the tiny, skinny black seed of the niger plant (*Guizotia abyssinica*), a golden-flowered sunflower relative. These tiny black seeds are high in fat and protein, draw goldfinches without fail, and also hold great appeal for house finches, purple finches, juncos, and siskins. Doves, house sparrows, and towhees may arrive to enjoy niger seeds, too. You can conduct

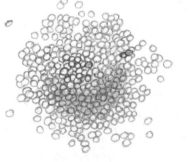

Clockwise from top left:
Black oil sunflower seed, niger, and millet are three of the best seeds for backyard birds.

your own informal inventory of customers by checking which birds are scratching for dropped niger below your tube feeders.

MILLET

Crunchy millet seeds are a high-protein food that's just the right size for the beaks of sparrows, juncos, bunting, and other small seed-eating birds. These tiny, round, golden or rusty brown seeds are a major ingredient in commercial birdseed mixes. Foxtail millet (*Setaria italica*) is the best millet for birds. It produces large seedheads, packed tightly with thousands of small, smooth kernels.

Sparrows love millet, and it's also favored by bobwhites, buntings,

> Some small to medium-size songbirds consume the equivalent of 80 to 100 percent of their body weight every day; for others, the amount is as little as 30 percent.

doves, juncos, quail, house sparrows, towhees, and Carolina wrens—the regular cast of characters at most feeding stations. Tanagers also devour millet. Should sunflower seeds be lacking at your feeder, cardinals, purple finches, goldfinches, grosbeaks, jays, and pine siskins will turn to millet.

If you're looking for a birdseed bargain, millet is a good choice.

Thistle Seed It's Not

NIGER (see the opposite page) has another name—thistle seed—that makes some birdwatchers hesitate to offer it in their feeders. They're afraid they'll end up with a yard full of prickly plants sprouting from the spilled seeds. But never fear—niger is not a thistle at all. It's the seed of niger plant (*Guizotia abyssinica*), an annual flower that's native to Ethiopia. Also, niger seed sold as birdseed is heated to prevent it from germinating because the plants can become pests in areas that have sunny, dry conditions.

Because it's so small and light-weight, you'll get zillions of seeds in a 50-pound sack, enough to take care of your small feeder birds for weeks.

It's also easy to start your own patch of millet for the birds to feast on. Just save some seeds out of a birdseed mix. In the spring when the soil warms, scatter the seeds on a sunny patch of loose soil. By late summer, you'll have a natural feeding place for small birds — and they'll thank you for it.

SAFFLOWER SEED

After niger, safflower seeds probably rank next in popularity among specialty seeds. Safflower seeds are white, pointed, plump seeds of a farm plant raised for oil production. The flowers that produce the seeds are an eye-catching bright orange, and often turn up in dried arrangements. They're easy to grow as annuals in a sunny garden.

If you love cardinals, you'll want to add safflower to your shopping list, as cardinals are the number-

High-protein millet, which you can find in commercial birdseed mixes, provides lots of energy for small seed-eating birds.

one customer for safflower seeds. Once the word gets out, you may find the number of cardinals at your diner increases daily, as long as you continue the handouts of oil-rich seeds. Doves, purple finches, grosbeaks, jays, and titmice may also partake. As with other unusual seeds, it may take a while to build a client base for safflower. Offer the seed sparingly at first, and be patient.

GRASS SEED

Small, narrow, bleached-tan grass seed is a great favorite of small seed-eating birds. Native sparrows and juncos—the same birds that eat most grass seeds in the wild—are the main customers for grass seed at the feeder. You may not be able to find grass seed in the birdseed aisle of your local discount store, but step across a few aisles to the lawn and garden

Low-Cost Food

CRACKED corn and chick scratch, a crushed feed of corn and other grains, are low-cost replacements for sunflower seeds and millet. If your budget is tight, you can augment the basics with one of these seeds—or you can switch to them entirely. Eliminating sunflowers and millet, however, may cause you to lose the loyalty of purple finches, goldfinches, and some other feeder birds, which may shift to your neighbor's feeder if their favorites are no longer on your menu.

Like coffee, chick scratch varies in the fineness of its grind, as various grades are manufactured to feed baby chicks of different ages. Ask your supplier for a coarse blend. The finely ground, almost powdery type tends to clump up into unpalatable lumps when it absorbs moisture, causing waste and inviting rodents to visit.

Cracked corn, too, may vary in the grind. Most suppliers don't mind if you ask to see a sample. A bag of cornmeal isn't much good for feeding birds for the same reasons that powdery chick scratch is inappropriate. Also, a fine-ground cornmeal doesn't attract larger-seed eaters. Coarsely cracked corn will satisfy the most customers.

department and you'll find all the 50-pound sacks you can carry. Smaller bags are easier to transport and will work as an occasional treat. Just remember to stock up on grass seed at the end of summer, before lawn-care products yield to Halloween candy and costumes. Be sure to check the label of the seed you're buying, and don't buy seed that's been chemically treated!

FLAXSEED

The shiny brown, flat oval seeds of flax are so high in oil, you can squeeze it out of them with a strong fingernail. Flaxseed can be expensive, so dole it out during rainy weather, when birds need extra energy. Nesting season—when birds are running themselves ragged bringing food to their young—is another good time to

Canary Seed

CANARY seed was very popular with caged-bird owners some 50 years ago, when singing canaries were resident pets in many kitchens and living rooms. As the popularity of these pets faded, the seed made a natural transition to wild birdseed mixes, where it remains popular with all the finch relatives of canaries. Goldfinches, purple finches, and house finches—as well as buntings, redpolls, and native sparrows—all eat canary seed.

Canary seed is a golden tan, smallish seed that you can buy by the pound or mixed with other choice seeds. The seed comes from a grass called canary grass (*Phalaris canariensis*), which has a notorious relative known as reedy canary grass (*P. arundinacea*), a fast-spreading plant that has become a pest in many areas, especially along water. Ducks, geese, quail and other game birds, and songbirds eat canary seed.

Feeder birds can be finicky about canary seed. At feeders in some regions they take to it readily, while at other feeders it may join the milo (also known as sorghum) and wheat kicked onto the ground in favor of choicer seeds. Do your own tests to determine whether your birds will take to canary seed by offering a small amount by itself or by checking to see if birds eat the canary seed when it's part of a seed mix.

offer flaxseed. Pine siskins, native sparrows, juncos, buntings, purple finches, house finches, goldfinches, and other finches are the main fans of flaxseed.

SEED MIXES

Not all seed mixes are created equal, and you can't judge a bag by its cover. Manufacturers decide what seeds to include and in what percentages, and the recipes vary widely from one supplier to another. The names of the mixes can be misleading, too: "Seed Mix Deluxe Blend" may be nothing special at all.

To make sure you buy a good product, examine the mix if the bag is transparent, or read the label. Laws require manufacturers to state the contents, listed in order of the most used to the least used. The lists usually include content percentages, too. Look for a high percentage of millet and sunflower, the top feeder favorites.

Additions of corn, wheat, and milo or sorghum often fill the balance of the bag. These inexpensive fillers cost much less per pound when you buy them as single-ingredient bags. As part of a mix, they add to the weight and jack up the price. Niger, flax, rapeseed, safflower, and canary grass, if they are included in small amounts, can be a bargain in a mix. But remember, with the exception of niger, your feeder birds may not readily accept these seeds.

WASTE-FREE MIXES

Bird feeding can be messy because hulls will rapidly accumulate on the ground beneath your feeders. Most people simply mulch over or scoop up the excess shells. But if you want things tidy or if you're feeding birds on a balcony, windowsill, or patio, a waste-free mix will keep the feeder area neat and clean.

Of course, the price per pound of these mixes is more than seeds with hulls. But every bit of what you're paying for is edible, and the convenience is worth a pretty penny itself.

Waste-free mixes usually include hull-less sunflower seeds (which you can also buy separately), plus bits of peanuts, finely cracked corn, and perhaps some canary seed, millet, or niger, which produce little waste. Compare the price per pound of this mix with the price of individual ingredients like sunflower chips, cracked corn, and chopped peanuts, and you may decide it's more cost-effective to make your own blend. Birds absolutely adore waste-free seed mixes, whether you buy them or stir them up yourself, because they don't have to work to eat the seeds. All large- and small-seed eaters relish the blend. Birds that don't usually eat seeds, such as bluebirds, catbirds, mockingbirds, robins, thrashers, and thrushes, also readily visit a feeder stocked with no-waste mix, where they can find an accessible, nutritious meal.

Treated Seed

TO boost the birdseed's value, manufacturers sometimes treat it with trace minerals or extra nutrients. This is usually unnecessary because birds don't eat only the seeds from your feeder. They also forage for wild foods, insects, and gravel that supply these needs naturally. But these treated seeds won't harm your birds.

Another treatment for birdseed is a great aid if squirrels and other animals are your nemeses. Capsaicin, the burning chemical of hot peppers, is effective at repelling animals from birdseed because it has the same effects on them as it does on us: burning mouth, watering eyes, and a nasty afterburn. Birds, interestingly enough, are completely unaffected. Treatment methods vary. Some seed brands are dusted with capsaicin powder, while others are soaked in a liquid extract that soaks into the seeds.

Use care when filling feeders with capsaicin-treated seed. Avoid getting the dust into your eyes or breathing it in. Wear rubber gloves to prevent the burning substance from contacting your skin. If you have small children that play in the yard, it may be better to turn to squirrel-proof feeders or other remedies than to fool with hot-pepper–treated birdseed. (The stuff may hurt your pets, too.)

Trimming the Birdseed Budget

ALTHOUGH welcoming a wide variety of birds to your backyard can be a joy, feeding so many hungry mouths (especially in winter) has the potential to put a serious dent in your wallet. To keep your feathered friends full while not breaking your bank, follow these guidelines: Limit the menu, and buy in bulk.

2 TRICKS

You really can get away with buying just a few different types of bird food to satisfy all your favorite birds. For example, cardinals, chickadees, jays, titmice, woodpeckers, and other strong-billed seed crackers love black oil sunflower. Smaller-seed eaters, such as finches, juncos, and sparrows, will dine on millet, while cracked corn is welcomed by blackbirds and starlings.

Buying in bulk can also help reduce the cost of feeding birds. That bag of birdseed you add to your cart in the grocery store can cost you about $1 a pound, whereas a 50-pound bag of sunflower seeds can costs less than 20 cents per pound. A big metal trash can is perfect for storing bulk birdseed and will also keep out freeloaders such as small rodents.

SIMPLE SAVERS

In addition to limiting the menu and buying in bulk, you can save on feeding birds in other ways. For example, buy chick scratch for cardinals, doves, quail, and other birds. (You can purchase chick scratch, which is inexpensive, at rural feed stores.) Stock up on birdseed when it's on sale, and store it in airtight containers until you need to use it. Or, make your own seed mixes instead of buying commercial products.

You can make more expensive seeds and nuts last longer by serving them in small, squirrel-proof feeders. Ration out treats like fruits and nuts in small quantities. And ask the produce manager at your local supermarket for free, discarded fruit.

Sunflower seed Niger Millet Flaxseed Berries Grapes Nuts Suet Nectar Bread food

Fruit at the Feeder

BIRDS' fondness for fruit gives backyard bird feeders another good way to tempt birds to feedings stations and the surrounding yard, particularly during midfall through winter, when the real thing is scarce. You can feed fresh, dried, and even frozen fruits to birds. Any fruit, from apples to figs, cherries to cactus, will have its takers at the feeder. Here's a look at some fruit favorites: apples, berries, grapefruit, grapes, melons, and oranges.

AN APPLE A DAY

If you roughly chop an apple into chunks and spread them in your feeder, you'll soon have jays, mockingbirds, and Carolina wrens nibbling away at the treasure. Scatter some chopped apple on the ground and robins, brown thrashers, and towhees may also partake of the feast. If bluebirds are in the area, they may fly in to enjoy a regular offering of apple.

Apples for the birds don't have to be perfect—they'll eagerly gobble up mushy or wormy fruit. Chopping an apple makes it easier for smaller beaks to eat, but slicing the fruit in half will attract customers, too, who will carefully eat every bit of flesh and leave just the hollowed-out skin behind.

Apples are also tops with starlings. Slice a couple of apples in

Chunks of apples at your feeder will bring in jays and wrens.

half and place them on the ground, and you'll get a starling circus outside your window, as the birds joust and squabble over the sweet flesh.

If you're trying to deter starlings from your feeding area, save your apples for feeders that they can't frequent. A coffee can hung horizontally, with a small entrance hole that allows titmice and chickadees to enter but bars starlings, is a good place to put a small amount of chopped apple. Weighted feeders that deter larger birds will also prevent starlings from getting your apple offerings. But since apples, especially those past their prime, are easy to come by (just ask your

> **Robins relish fruit, including apples. But the robins you spot in May may not be the same ones you see in November. Many robins from far north migrate to spend the winter in less frigid states, while the summertime inhabitants there head farther south.**

grocer), you can also include starlings in this feast. Slice whole fruits in half and place them in a decoy feeder, away from those that your more desirable birds frequent.

Too Many Apples?

IF you find yourself with an abundance of apples and no room in the fridge for storage, take time to slice and dry them for later use. You don't have to remove the cores—birds like the seeds, too. Just slice the apples thinly with a sharp knife, and loosely string the slices with a heavy-duty carpet needle and thread. Hang the slices to dry.

You can also spread the slices on cookie sheets and bake them at 200°F. How long they take to dry in the oven depends on the moisture content and thickness of the apple slices. Check the slices after 15 minutes, then increase the time as needed by 10-minute intervals. Store dried apples in resealable plastic bags. Chop or serve whole in feeders, or use strings of dried apple slices to decorate outdoor evergreens or a discarded Christmas tree.

> **Birds aren't particular about what variety of strawberry you plant. Their sharp beaks can easily nip a slice out of even the biggest strawberry, while small wild (*Fragaria vesca*) or alpine strawberries (*F. montana fraga*) go down the hatch whole.**

BRINGING 'EM IN WITH BERRIES

Berries are one of the big reasons for dramatic declines in bird traffic at feeders in the summertime. Even premium birdseed can't compare to the temptation of ripening blackberries (*Rubus* spp.), blueberries (*Vaccinium* spp.), huckleberries (*Gaylussacia* spp.), mulberries (*Morus* spp.), salmonberries (*Rubus spectabilis*), and dozens of other kinds of wild and cultivated berries.

You'd think that since birds are this attracted to berries, they'd come like magic to a feeder full of these favorites. But berries offer that kind of draw only if you offer them at times when they aren't available from other sources. If you find yourself with extra berries of any kind in summer, such as the last few strawberries in the box, don't bother putting them in the feeder. You'll probably get no takers when nature's bounty is all around. Instead, pop your leftover spring, summer, and fall berries into a plastic bag or container and freeze them. In wintertime, the birds will gobble up bruised or battered berry bits as if they were rare treasures.

Gather berry-laden branches of dogwoods (*Cornus* spp.), hawthorns (*Crataegus* spp.), hollies (*Illex* spp.), cedars (*Juniperus* spp.), or other bird favorites, and offer them in a tray feeder. (For information on growing your own fruit for the birds, see pages 142 and 148.)

GOING FOR GRAPEFRUIT

Ruby red or pale golden, grapefruits are great additions to the bird-feeder banquet. Filled with their own luscious, juicy pulp, they may attract the attention of chickadees, house finches, mockingbirds, robins, and other birds. Orioles may sample the flesh, though sweet oranges tempt these birds more easily. Emptied of the contents—by you or the birds—grapefruit rind halves make sturdy, simple mini-feeders for filling with bacon fat, melted suet, or other offerings.

Grapefruit is also a suitable distraction for starlings, which may forsake the main feeder area for an offering of grapefruit halves in easy reach. You can put the halved fruit into wire baskets (a suet feeder usually fits; for more information on suet feeders, see page 71), or impale a half-grapefruit on a sturdy nail—either horizontally, for perchers such as starlings and mockingbirds, or vertically, for clinging birds such as chickadees.

Make feeder baskets from empty grapefruit halves by sticking a wire through the rind at three equidistant points, about ¼ inch from the top. Twist the wires together and suspend from a tree branch or shepherd's crook. Chopped apples, raisins, currants, sunflower seeds, or peanuts are good to serve in grapefruit baskets. The edge of the rind makes a serviceable perch for lightweight birds such as chickadees.

Serving Up Blueberries

SAVE some blueberries to put in your feeder in fall and winter, times when natural fruit is hard to find. You can freeze or dry fresh berries for later use. To dry blueberries, spread them on a window screen in full summer sun, covered by a layer of gauze or cheesecloth to keep bugs away. Support the screen on blocks so that air can circulate on all sides of the berries.

Unless you're in the blueberry business, your stock will most likely be small. Dole them out a scant handful at a time so that they aren't wasted. Bluebirds, mockingbirds, robins, brown thrashers, woodpeckers, and Carolina wrens may be tempted by the handout. Many of these blueberry-eating birds prefer fruit, mealworms, peanut-butter dough, and other soft goodies to birdseed. To cut down on competition for feeder space, scatter the blueberries in an open tray feeder that you reserve for soft foods.

Sunflower seed Niger Millet Flaxseed Berries Grapes Nuts Suet Nectar Bread **food**

ATTENTION-GRABBING GRAPES

Grapevines are great vines, as far as birds are concerned. Like other rampant-growing vines, grapes offer good cover, shelter from the elements, and protected nesting spots. Their fruit is a favorite of cardinals, catbirds, great crested flycatchers, grosbeaks, mockingbirds, tanagers, thrashers, thrushes, woodpeckers, wrens . . . and lots more. Their sweet-smelling flowers attract a myriad of tiny bugs—which supplies more fodder for foraging birds. And the peeling bark of their vines is easy for birds to strip and use for nest weaving.

If you didn't inherit Grandma's grape arbor, start your own on a strong trellis by planting a fast-growing, easy-care 'Concord' vine if you live in the North (Zones 5 to 8), or a muscadine if you're a southern gardener (Zones 7 to 9). In 2 years, you'll have a decent crop.

In the meantime, while your vine grows, get your grapes from other sources. Salvage any strays from your refrigerator fruit bin; birds don't mind withered fruit. Place single grapes in an open tray feeder for easy visibility, preferably in the soft-foods feeder so that grape lovers don't have to compete with seed eaters for feeder space.

Like other fruits, grapes attract the most attention from birds in fall

Grow grapes in your backyard and you're sure to catch the attention of fruit lovers, like this mockingbird.

and winter, when natural fruit is scarce. But if you have fruit eaters such as bluebirds, catbirds, mockingbirds, or Carolina wrens nesting in or near your yard, you may enjoy a steady stream of customers to your fruit feeders through the summer, especially if there's no natural fruit nearby.

Since birds are creatures of habit, it's a good idea to put grapes in the same spot if you offer them regularly. Hang clusters of grapes on hooks or nails, or fasten them on branches of shrubs or trees. To prevent these watery, thin-skinned fruits from freezing to snow or frozen soil, freeze a supply of individual grapes in resealable plastic bags for winter use. After winter snow or ice storms, chop grapes coarsely (whole frozen grapes are

Dried Grapes

RAISINS are delicious treats for birds that like to eat fruit, but it may take some ingenuity on your part to launch a raisin-feeding campaign. Mockingbirds, bluebirds, robins, tanagers, thrushes, and other birds that eat mainly soft foods are the best customers for raisins, but these birds aren't regulars at bird feeders. They're used to plucking fruits from the branches of plants rather than from a feeder.

Instead of sprinkling raisins in a feeder, try incorporating them into a mix of other soft foods these birds would enjoy. Keep a small open-tray feeder just for these customers, where you can experiment with various foods and recipes to see which one gets the most takers. If birds don't discover the raisins within a week or so, try making a "raisin tree." Choose a shrub or tree with stiff, slender, twiggy branches, such as a plum tree. Impale raisins on the branch tips, using as many of the tiny fruits as you have the patience to attach. Once the birds discover the raisins, you can draw their attention further by scattering the raisins on the ground near the "raisin tree."

For the best bargain, look for raisins in bulk bins at the grocery or health-food store, where they usually cost much less per pound than commercial-brand boxes. Store extras in your refrigerator.

too big to swallow), and scatter them on the ground for robins and other birds to scoop up.

MOUTH-WATERING MELONS

Every time you scrape seeds out of a melon, you're throwing away a healthy snack for your feathered friends. Cardinals, doves, grackles, jays, nuthatches, sparrows, titmice, and woodpeckers eagerly devour the dried seeds of any kind of melon: cantaloupe, honeydew, watermelon, or even fancy French 'Charantais'.

If you want to add melons to your feeder menu, you'll find that the seeds dry quickly and easily on an old window screen supported on lawn chairs. Scoop out the seeds and rinse them in a colander to remove any clinging bits of pulp. Spread the seeds out on the screen, and crumble the clumps occasionally as they dry to keep them from sticking together. If you want to save the seeds for fall and winter feeding, cover them with a single

Pumpkin and Squash Seeds

THE nutty innards of pumpkins and squash are delectable to many seed-eating birds, including cardinals, jays, nuthatches, titmice, and woodpeckers. These vegetables usually produce a generous quantity of seeds, providing a ready source of free bird food to add to your feeder offerings. Pumpkins and squash are fall and winter crops, which is perfect timing because that's when feeders are at their busiest. (For tips on preparing the seeds, see "Mouth-Watering Melons" on this page.)

Like other unusual foods, the seeds may sit unnoticed in your feeder for a few days before birds begin to sample them. Scatter a few of the light-colored seeds in an open tray of black sunflower seeds to help the birds spot them more easily.

Chipmunks, squirrels, and other furry feeder visitors also delight in eating pumpkin and squash seeds. If you have separate feeders for squirrels and other wildlife, add these seeds to the menu.

thickness of cheesecloth to keep birds from nibbling on the seeds while they dry. Pour the dried seeds into brown paper bags and store them in metal containers.

If you buy a melon in winter, wash the pulp off the seeds in a colander, shake off excess water, spread the seeds on a section of newspaper, and dry on top of the refrigerator or another warm place. Turn the seeds daily to prevent mold from developing. Or you can save time and just scrape the fresh seeds into the feeder for birds to sort out themselves.

FRESH ORANGES

The fructose in oranges (and some other fruits) is apparently what tempts orioles and house finches to oranges offered at the feeding station. These birds are also fond of sugar-water served in nectar feeders. Cardinals, mockingbirds, robins, starlings, woodpeckers, and, if you're lucky, bluebirds also will partake of this citrusy treat.

Commercially made orange feeders make it a snap to serve a fresh halved orange to your guests. You can also make your own feeder from a scrap of wood and a stout nail. Mount the feeder horizontally on a deck railing or flat-topped post, or hang it vertically. The birds will reach the orange either way.

You can feed oranges year-round with good results. Spring migrant orioles, just back in breeding territory or passing through, are often quick to home in on an orange feeder. If you haven't had orioles at your feeding station before, be patient. It may take the birds a while to find the fruit. Replace the orange as necessary if patrons are slow in arriving.

Tempt Baltimore orioles to your yard with a tasty offering of fresh orange halves.

Common Foods

Q I use a lot of eggs on a weekly basis, and while I know I can add the shells to my compost pile, I was wondering if they'd also work as a feeder food for birds. What do you think?

A Leftover eggshells are a good source of calcium for egg-laying female birds in later winter and early spring. They need the calcium to strengthen the shells of their own eggs and the developing bones of the chicks within.

So yes, you can add eggshells to the menu. Small, crushed pieces of eggshell (crush them with a rolling pin) are the easiest for birds to eat. Sprinkle the crushed shells in a tray feeder, in a spot that's separate from birdseed, so that birds who want the crushed shells won't have to compete with a crowd of seed eaters.

Q I love nuts and would like to plant some nut trees in my backyard. Any advice on good nut tree choices that will satisfy both me and the birds?

A Hickory nuts and hazelnuts are two top choices. Hickories (*Carya* spp.) grow in Zones 3 to 8, their foliage turns a rich gold in the fall, and their nuts are a winter staple of woodpeckers. Bushy filberts or hazelnuts (*Corylus* spp.) have delicious, easy-to-crack nuts. They grow in Zones 2 to 8 and make an excellent hedge when planted in rows.

Q How can I keep birds from eating my prized sweet corn? I've a tried a scarecrow, but even so, the birds seem to eat more corn than I do!

A Those sweet, milky kernels of corn are prime fodder for blackbirds, jays, and, of course, crows. A scarecrow is the classic solution for hungry birds in the garden, but it works only until the birds figure out it's not human. You can make the effect last a little longer by including moving elements—such as long shirtsleeves or streamers that flap in the breeze—and a Halloween latex mask with human features.

Nuts and Such

NUTS are extra-rich in fat as well as in protein—exactly the kind of snack hungry birds crave. Jays, titmice, chickadees, woodpeckers, and, of course, nuthatches are just crazy about nuts. They peck at them on the spot or carry them off to store for later use. Nuts, however, carry a hefty price tag at the store. At $5 a pound and up, walnuts, almonds, pecans, and other nuts can break the bird-feeding bank in a big hurry. Still, a spread of nuts in the feeder is guaranteed to attract a wonderful array of birds. And nothing works as well as nuts for hand-taming these birds (see "Hand-Feeding" on page 77 for more information).

Walnuts and other members of the *Juglans* genus have evolved a highly effective way of making sure their species survives: Their roots exude a toxin called juglone that stunts or kills many plants growing near the tree.

BUYING AND STORING

You'll find the best prices on nuts through food co-ops, at health-food stores, and in the bulk-foods aisle of your grocery store, where you can fill a bag with your selections. At the grocery store, packaged nuts are often put on sale in time for Christmas baking. Unsalted, uncoated raw nuts are best. In other words, buy the plain, raw almonds, not the sugar-coated, pastel-colored dessert variety.

Nuts contain a lot of oil, which can turn rancid in warm weather or room-temperature storage. Should your stockpile of nuts go bad, pour them into a feeder and let the birds decide for themselves whether they're past the eating stage.

Birds welcome nuts year-round, but save most of them to feed in cold weather, when birds most need high-fat, high-calorie foods. To give the birds a treat, fill a tube sock with nuts, hold the end closed, and give it a few good whacks with a hammer. Empty the sock into a tray feeder, then sit back and watch the birds.

SERVING UP WALNUTS

Walnuts are a welcome treat for many birds, including chickadees, jays, nuthatches, titmice, and woodpeckers. Of course, your bushy-tailed "friends" also adore them, and that means you'll want to dole them out a bit at a time to prevent squirrels or chipmunks from skedaddling with bulging cheeks, leaving a suspiciously empty feeder in their wake.

Birds will quickly snatch up big walnut pieces, but they will fly away from the feeder to a tree limb or other protected spot where they can eat the meat bit by bit. If you want the birds to linger, use a rolling pin to break the nuts into smaller chunks before you put them in your feeders. If you'd rather sharpen your skills at bird watching away from the feeder, put out larger pieces and follow the birds with your eyes or binoculars as they fly off to a tree, and then watch them break the nut down to size.

Shelled nuts are best at the feeder (although birds also appreciate broken pieces of walnuts still in the shell). Shelled walnuts are widely available, but you'll generally find the best prices at supermarket bulk-food bins or through co-ops or health-food stores.

Hunting for Nuts

HERE'S an easy way to acquire lots of nuts for nothing, plus develop a new family tradition at the same time: Go nut hunting. No matter where you live, some kind of wild nut trees are bound to be within picking distance.

Many suburban and country roads are still dotted with fine nut trees, and others grow in fields, hedgerows, and woods. You'll have to search out the tree and get permission to pick the nuts. Don't gather nuts without asking permission first—an altercation with an unhappy landowner will make the family outing memorable, and not in a good way!

After the expedition, spread your booty in shallow cardboard boxes in an airy, dry place—like your garage. After the hulls have dried (or fallen off, in some cases), pour the nuts into mouse-proof containers for storage.

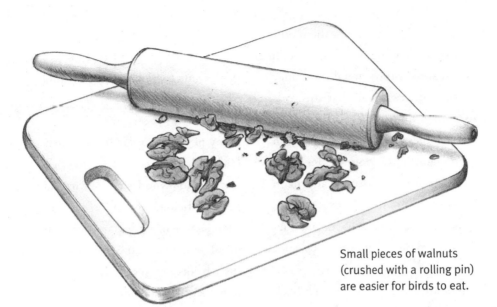

Small pieces of walnuts
(crushed with a rolling pin)
are easier for birds to eat.

BELOVED ACORNS

Packed with protein, acorns are a huge hit with all nut-eating birds, including chickadees, jays, nuthatches, titmice, and woodpeckers. They're also tops with game birds like wild turkeys and quail. Lacking the necessary whacking power to get at acorn nutmeats themselves, smaller birds such as buntings, finches, juncos, and sparrows will clean up crumbs dropped by larger birds.

Oak (*Quercus* spp.) trees of any kind are magnets for birds when the acorns are ripe for picking, which may be late summer to fall, depending on the oak species.

Beating the birds to the harvest may sound a little mean, but you're really just stockpiling acorns for winter feeding, when acorns can be hard to find.

It doesn't take a lot of effort to gather a generous supply of acorns for winter bird feeding. Just fill your pockets whenever you notice the fallen nuts on your nature hikes or while strolling your yard. Although some acorns taste sweet to human palates and others are extremely bitter, birds seem to appreciate all of them.

Some acorns begin to germinate soon after hitting the ground, while others need a rest period over winter before they sprout. To keep

Sunflower seed• Niger• Millet• Flaxseed• Berries• Grapes• Nuts• Suet• Nectar• Bread

your acorns fresh, store them out-doors or in an unheated garage in a moisture-proof metal container with a secure lid, so that squirrels or other animal pests don't help themselves to your hoard. When you want to give your feeder birds a treat, put a handful of acorns in an old sock, fold over the top, place the sock on a hard, flat sur-face, and use a hammer to split open the acorns. Pour the broken nuts into a tray feeder and sit back to watch the show.

A nighttime offering of walnuts, spread in a feeder after dark (especially in fall and winter), may bring you the enchanting surprise of a flying squirrel in your feeder. These gentle, dark-eyed creatures are unusually fearless around humans, and if you approach quietly, they will let you watch close up while they eat. They're particularly fond of walnuts.

THE POWER OF PEANUTS

Peanuts (which aren't true nuts, by the way—they're legumes) make a nutritious mouthful for many of your regular feeder birds. Chickadees, jays, nuthatches, tit-mice, and woodpeckers are all peanut aficionados. Other visitors, such as juncos and sparrows, may nibble smaller peanut pieces, but their beaks are generally too small to get a grip on a large kernel.

You can actually grow peanuts in your garden, although if you live in the northern half of the country, you'll need to choose fast-maturing varieties. Plant peanuts in the spring and harvest in the fall when the plants' leaves turn yellow.

Of course, you can also buy peanuts to feed to your birds, and that's what most people do. Check the bulk-food bins at supermarkets or health-food stores for bargain-priced peanuts—they may cost less than those sold especially for bird feeding. Unsalted peanuts, either in or out of the shell, are the best choice for birds, although birds will also gobble the salted variety. That extra-heavy dose of sodium won't harm your birds, but be sure water is freely available to slake their thirst. Roasted and raw peanuts seem to be equally popular.

Whichever type of peanuts you offer, be sure to buy fresh stock. Old peanuts may be rancid and unpalatable. When in doubt, try a couple yourself. If the peanuts taste good and nutty to you, your birds will devour them like kids at a baseball game.

In addition to peanuts, you might also hear about birders offering peanut hearts to their feathered friends. Peanut hearts sound like they're the best part of the peanut, but the opposite is true. Peanut hearts are a by-product of peanut-butter manufacturing, removed before the peanuts are processed.

You'll find peanut hearts at some bird-supply stores and as an ingredient in some bagged "premium" seed mixes.

PEANUT BUTTER

Peanut butter is a perfect bird food: It's ultrahigh in fat and full of protein, which makes it a super food for cold-weather feeding

Foiling Peanut Thieves

ONE way to outsmart squirrels and chipmunks (who also love peanuts) is to be stingy: Dole out a handful of peanuts at a time on fall and winter mornings, when the feeders are hopping with birds. Your presence should send squirrels scurrying, which is just enough time for the birds to swoop in and grab a nutty snack. By the time the squirrels return, all that's left of the peanuts will be a tantalizing aroma.

You can make your own squirrel-resistant peanut feeder by covering a shallow tray feeder with a piece of strong ½-inch wire mesh. However, squirrels may still spend hours trying to wrest the wire from the wood, and their presence will discourage birds. If that is the case, invest in a sturdy "large seed" feeder made of metal, with a heavy-duty wire cage surrounding a central tube feeder. The wire allows birds easy access to the peanuts but blocks squirrels from reaching the tasty treats.

(when birds need extra calories), and a real treat any time of year. Bluebirds, chickadees, jays, nuthatches, starlings, titmice, woodpeckers, and Carolina wrens all love peanut butter.

The main drawback to feeding peanut butter is the expense (if you offer it as a regular menu item) — but that's a challenge that's easy to overcome.

Birds aren't fussy about brands, so buy the cheapest peanut butter you can find. To stretch your peanut butter, mix it with fillers like cornmeal or rolled oats (½ cup of peanut butter mixed into 2 cups uncooked cornmeal or rolled oats).

Spoon the mixture onto a tray feeder and stand back as birds flock to the feast. Offer peanut butter or peanut butter mixtures in small amounts to prevent your treasured treat from being devoured before your eyes by starlings or squirrels and other rodents. Put out only what the birds will eat in an hour or so. You can always renew the feeding later.

PEAS

Dried peas are a favorite food for doves, grouse, quail, pheasants, and large songbirds, including cardinals and grosbeaks. If you live

A Pinch of Cornmeal

HIGH in fat and protein, cornmeal is the perfect foundation for bird-attracting recipes. It's impractical for feeding alone because it quickly absorbs moisture and becomes rancid if uneaten. You can try sprinkling cornmeal lightly over snow-covered ground for doves, juncos, native sparrows, towhees, and other ground-feeding birds.

Mix cornmeal with peanut butter to extend that expensive spread so that is serves more birds and slides down their gullets more easily. Combine the two at a 1:1 ratio and stuff into holes drilled in a section of 3- to 4-inch-diameter log. Use a heavy-duty screw eye in one end of the log to hang it from a branch. This makes an easy feeder that's irresistible to chickadees, nuthatches, titmice, and woodpeckers.

near game-bird habitat, you can grow peas for fall and winter food right in place. A planting of peas will provide long-lasting food for foraging quail and other game birds. However, in order to provide a bountiful harvest for the birds when the peas mature, you'll have to discourage other birds from eating the seeds at planting time. Blackbirds, crows, grackles, jays, and English sparrows have an uncanny knack for finding a newly planted pea patch. To prevent them from robbing the seeds, cover the planting area with floating row cover or a layer of straw.

Many suppliers treat pea seeds with chemicals, so be sure to ask for untreated seed when you purchase your peas. You'll have to look a little harder for untreated bulk seeds, but they are available. Check mail-order sources (see "Resources and Recommended Reading" on page 202), or ask local seed suppliers, especially Mom & Pop hardware stores in rural areas or at farm supply stores. Or you can try planting a plastic bag of dried soup peas from the supermarket. (Use whole peas, not split peas, because split peas won't germinate.)

PLANTING PEAS
at a glance

To grow a small patch of a peas, prepare the soil as you would for any annual plant:

1. Remove vegetation.

2. Turn the soil.

3. Rake to a moderately fine texture.

4. Scatter pea seeds thickly over the bed.

5. Cover the pea seeds with enough soil that the seeds don't grab the attention of blackbirds.

At the feeder, birds often overlook dry peas in favor of the ever-popular sunflower seeds and other offerings. If you scatter a handful of dry peas among a tray of black sunflower seeds, the eye-catching white seeds may draw the attention of woodpeckers.

Another way to encourage wild birds to shift to eating a new food like dried peas or small dried beans is to wait until the feeders are almost empty and then put out about a cupful of the peas in place of the sunflower seeds that would normally fill the feeder. Once the birds get a taste for the new food, usually within a day, you can return to the regular food and mix the dried legumes among them.

You also can place dried peas in a low tray feeder or directly on the ground for doves, pheasants, and other ground feeders, or in open tray feeders for cardinals and grosbeaks.

PARTRIDGE PEA

Peas and beans belong to the plant group called legumes, which also includes perennial flowers and even some shrubs and trees. Nearly all game birds like to eat a variety of legume seeds. Partridge pea (*Cassia fasciculata*, also known as *Chamaecrista fasciculata*), a pretty yellow-flowered perennial legume, is a particular favorite of quail. It's easy to add this perennial to your wildflower meadow or prairie garden, where it will add late-season color and winter-long food. Partridge pea is hardy to Zone 5. It may bloom the first year from an early sowing, but it usually requires two full seasons to perform; if you live in Zone 3 or 4, you can take your chances and try it anyway, mulching deeply with fall leaves to help it live through the winter deep freeze.

Gradually introduce dried peas to birds by offering them with a mix of other food, such as sunflower seeds.

Common Foods

Q Will adding red dye to hummingbird nectar make the birds sick? Or is that an old wives' tale?

A Old wives' tale it is. No scientific studies exist that indicate a negative effect on hummingbirds from red dye. However, you don't need to waste your time adding red dye to their nectar because colored nectar doesn't attract any more hummingbirds than clear nectar, as long as there's a bit of red plastic near the feeding ports.

Q I'm planning to take an extended vacation this spring. Will the birds that have come to depend on my feeders starve since I won't be around to feed them?

A They won't starve, although they may have a hard time for a while until they locate other food sources. The exception, though, is in winter. Low temps and a scarcity of natural food during a hard winter take a toll on birds, and a full feeder can mean the difference between life and death.

Q Is it really okay to feed birds peanut butter? I'm afraid that since it's so thick, birds will choke on it. What do you think?

A Experts at Cornell University say it's perfectly safe to feed peanut butter to birds straight. If you don't want to take chances, though, you can mix peanut butter with cornmeal or rolled oats. (See "Peanut Butter" on page 43 for more information.)

Q I'd like to grow my own birdseed, but it seems like I'd have to plant a lot of seed to get a reasonable amount. Do you have any suggestions for an easy way to grow seed for the birds?

A Try buying lettuce seed and planting several crops in a big batch. Let it go to seed, then lay the stalks of ripe seeds in an open tray feeder for finch treats. And planting several rows of giant sunflowers will give you armloads of seedheads that you can tie to a post and let the birds pick off.

Suet and Nectar

FROM a bird's point of view, suet is perfect. Because their metabolism is set on fast-forward, birds never have to worry about eating too many calories. A ready supply of calories from solid suet helps birds conserve precious energy. That's important because birds use up tremendous amounts of calories in their never-ending search for insects, seeds, and other foods.

Nectar is the reward that bees and beneficial insects, as well as hummingbirds, seek when they buzz from one blossom to the next. As they collect nectar, the insects also collect pollen and pollinate the flowers. Tubular flowers, like those of honeysuckle and trumpet vines, are typically rich in nectar.

THE SKINNY ON SUET

True suet is the white fat surrounding cow or sheep kidneys, but the term is generally used to include other animal fat, which birds like just as well. Prepackaged slabs, wrapped in plastic and purified so they stay fresh for a long time, are the most convenient form of suet. At about a dollar or two apiece, they are a great buy, lasting for several weeks in the feeder, depending on the traffic.

Added Ingredients

YOU'LL find suet blocks with fruit, suet with nuts, and suet with seed offered for sale. Sounds tempting—just keep in mind that suet alone is enough of a draw to attract all kinds of birds without other enticements.

Steer clear of suet that includes birdseed mix, such as millet and other small seeds. The main customers for fat don't eat these seeds, and the ground-feeding birds that do eat the seeds don't visit suet cages. Also, birds can get their feathers greasy if they try to reach in for the seeds, which may affect the vital insulation properties of their plumage.

You can also buy beef trimmings from the supermarket and stockpile them in the freezer so you always have a good supply on hand. Ask at your local meat counter for beef trimmings, and you may get the precious fat for free or quite cheaply. Some butchers will grind the fat for you if you ask, which makes it easier to include in recipes or offer to birds that have a hard time clinging to wire feeders, such as bluebirds and native sparrows. (You may also be able to buy true suet, although it is more expensive than plain old fat.) You can pour bacon grease, beef drippings, or other melted fat into washed cat-food or tuna cans for quick fat feeders, as well. (Just punch a hole in the can and attach a wire for hanging.)

You don't have to melt suet or fat before offering it to birds—they'll eat it in a solid form. If you're working with true suet or beef trimmings, just slice off chunks or strips with a stout chef's knife and fill your containers. Plastic mesh bags from onions are great for instant suet feeders: Just fill the empty mesh bag with fat, tie the top closed, and hang from a branch, hook, or nail.

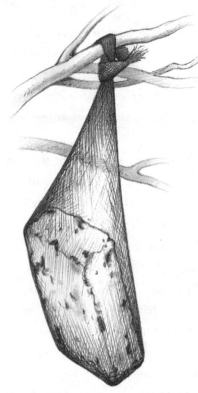

You don't need to buy a special feeder for suet—a plastic mesh onion bag works great.

Most suet feeders hang near eye level, but many ground-feeding birds also like some fat in their diets. To accommodate these guests, feed chopped suet in a tray feeder near ground level.

BIRDS AND BACON

In the old days when bacon was a regular part of breakfast, cooks were happy to share the leftover grease with their feathered friends.

In today's fat-conscious society, many people have sworn off bacon, but birds don't need to fight fat.

The simplest way to package bacon grease for bird feeding is in metal tuna or cat-food cans. Punch a hole in the side wall of the can with a nail. Use pliers to bend the tips of a wire into a knot that won't slip through the hole, and thread the wire through the can for hanging. Fill the can to the brim with cooled but still-liquid bacon grease, then stick it in the refrigerator to solidify. Once the grease is no longer runny, hang the can from a branch.

Bluebirds, jays, woodpeckers, and Carolina wrens readily accept this source of fat, whether you offer it straight or use it in bird-treat recipes. Bacon grease also draws crows, starlings, and even ravens.

NOURISHING NECTAR

Homemade nectar is nothing more than a solution of sugar and water, but when you offer it in a plastic feeder, it's irresistible to hummingbirds. Nectar feeders, particularly those with orange trim, also attract orioles; house finches, warblers, woodpeckers, and other species are also making increasing use of nectar feeders.

To make nectar, bring 2 or 3 cups of water to a boil in a small saucepan. Stir in ½ cup of white

Summer Suet Feeding

ALTHOUGH the number of suet customers peaks in winter, suet and fat are popular all year long. Keep in mind, though, that suet and fat can melt quickly in the heat of summer. This is the time when feeding purified blocks makes sense, as they're very slow to melt or turn rancid in warm weather. If you're feeding your own collection of fats, keep the offerings small so that the stuff stays palatable. Move feeders to the shade or keep them out of direct sun to slow the melting. For a more solid, slower-melting product, heat fat and suet over low heat on the stove, discard the bottom layer of particles in the pan, and use only the top layer to fill feeders.

granulated sugar. Continue stirring until the sugar is dissolved. Cool the solution and pour it into a clean hummingbird feeder. Don't use honey to make nectar—it's sweet, but it can cause bacterial and fungal diseases in hummingbirds.

If you're trying to attract hummingbirds for the first time, use the more concentrated version of the formula (½ cup sugar to 2 cups water). There's no need to add food coloring to the syrup (see the first question on page 47). Once you have regular customers at your feeders, reduce the sweetness of your homemade nectar because that's better for the birds' long-term health.

If you feed birds homemade nectar, keep in mind that nectar breeds bacteria easily, especially in warm weather. Be sure to empty your feeders twice weekly. Clean each feeder by pouring boiling water through it, then refill with fresh solution. To learn more about hummingbird nectar feeders, turn to page 71.

A mixture of sugar and water in a nectar feeder is all you need to attract this Bullock's oriole to your yard.

SNITCHING A SNIP

More than 60 species of birds—besides hummingbirds—have been seen snitching a sip of sugar water from nectar feeders. Check your feeders frequently to see who's visiting yours. The most common non-hummingbird guests are orioles and house finches, with woodpeckers close behind. Also look for these species:

- Cardinals
- Chickadees
- Goldfinches
- Black-headed grosbeaks
- Jays
- Tanagers
- Titmice
- Downy woodpeckers

Cereal, Dog Food, Doughnuts—And More

OUR feathered friends like to mix it up now and then with a taste of the unusual, instead of just feasting on standard fare. Cereal, bread, dog food, and doughnuts all appeal to a variety of birds—and adding these extras to your avian menu is a good way to use up leftover and stale products that would otherwise go to waste.

BREAKING BREAD

Ounce for ounce, even fortified bread can't compare to the food value of sunflower and other bird seeds, which offer the high-fat, high-protein diet that birds need.

> **Although ducks and geese at public ponds are usually quick to grab bread from your fingers, wild ducks and geese have little interest in bread because they're not accustomed to getting such handouts.**

But bread is a fine addition to any feeding program—jays, magpies, mockingbirds, robins, native sparrows, Carolina wrens, and many other species will quickly gobble it up. Bread also brings in blackbirds, grackles, house sparrows, and starlings—so if you're trying to discourage these birds, think twice before adding it to the menu. Squirrels, ground squirrels, and chipmunks, as well as raccoons, opossums, and dogs, also eat bread.

Birds will pretty much eat any kind of bread. As long as you're not feeding your bird guests a bread-only menu, you needn't worry whether it offers great nutrition. A stale slice of refined white bread is just as welcome to hungry birds as a fresh loaf of all-natural multigrain bread. Crumble the bread into small bits to make it easy for doves, sparrows, and other small-beaked birds to eat. Feeding bread as crumbs also keeps birds lingering at your feeder, instead of allowing them to fly off with a big chunk to eat out of your sight.

To avoid waste, offer bread in small amounts at the feeder until you can gauge how quickly the birds will eat it. (It's best to use a roofed feeder because bread quickly turns moldy if it gets wet. If bread does get wet, throw it out as soon as you can.) Freeze leftovers for later use. Keep frozen bread, crumbled in resealable plastic bags, on hand for emergencies like snowstorms, when any bluebirds, robins, or other thrushes in the area will be grateful for a handout of this nutritious food.

Because bread is soft and absorbent, it's ideal for soaking up bacon fat, melted suet, beef drippings from a roast or broiler pan, and other oils. Chickadees, jays, titmice, woodpeckers, and many other birds will accept such high-

Baking Bread

IF you like to bake, you can try making special bread just for birds. Add liberal doses of the following ingredients, in any combination, to your dough before baking. These special breads attract more takers than a standard loaf of white bread.

Acorn nutmeats

Acorn or winter squash seeds

Almonds, chopped

Apples, chopped or coarsely grated

Beechnut nutmeats

Blueberries, fresh or dried

Buckwheat kernels

Canned whole-kernel corn

Cantaloupe seeds

Cherries, fresh or dried

Currants

Grapes, chopped

Hickory nuts

Hulled sunflower chips

Millet, whole

Oatmeal

Oranges, chopped

Pasta, leftover cooked, any kind, chopped if large

Peaches, chopped

Peanut butter, chunky

Peanuts, raw or roasted

Pears, chopped

Pecans, chopped

Pine nuts

Plums, chopped

Pumpkin seeds

Raisins

Strawberries

Walnuts, chopped

Watermelon seeds

Sunflower seed Niger Millet Flaxseed Berries Grapes Nuts Suet Nectar Bread

food

fat offerings eagerly, especially in cold weather when they need the extra energy. Cut the bread into cubes or crumble it into cool but still-liquid fat, and serve in a large, shallow plastic tray to avoid grease stains on wood bird feeders.

CEREAL: BIRD BREAKFAST

Hungry birds in your backyard will change your whole perspective on stale cereal—instead of seeing that inch or two at the bottom as a waste of good food, turn it into a

---

Quick Reference | **SHARING LEFTOVER CEREAL**

CHECK out the chart below to find out how to prepare cereals or mix them with other foods, what type of feeder to put various cereals in, and what birds these grainy treats will please.

CEREAL TYPE	HOW TO PREPARE	HOW TO SERVE	DESIRABLE BIRDS ATTRACTED
Bran flakes	Crush with a rolling pin.	Ground feeder	Doves, juncos, quail, pheasants, native sparrows
Cheerios	Offer whole.	Tray feeder	Blackbirds, chickadees, jays, mockingbirds, titmice
Corn flakes	Crush with a rolling pin.	Ground feeder	Blackbirds, buntings, doves, juncos, pheasants, quail
	Crush with a rolling pin; mix each cup cereal with ¼ cup peanut butter, peanut oil, bacon drippings, meat drippings, or melted suet to make a crumbly mix.	Tray feeder	Cardinals, chickadees, jays, nuthatches, titmice, woodpeckers, wrens
Crisped rice	Mix each cup cereal with ¼ cup peanut butter, peanut oil, bacon drippings, or meat drippings.	Tray feeder	Cardinals, chickadees, jays, nuthatches, titmice, woodpeckers
Fruit/nut cereals	Crush lightly with a rolling pin to break up flakes.	Ground feeder	Buntings, robins, thrushes, towhees, native sparrows
		Tray feeder	Cardinals, chickadees, jays, nuthatches, titmice, woodpeckers, wrens
Hot cereals	Mix each cup cereal with ¼ cup peanut butter, peanut oil, bacon drippings, or meat drippings.	Tray feeder	Cardinals, chickadees, jays, nuthatches, titmice, woodpeckers
Puffed rice	—	—	Not appealing to birds
Shredded wheat	Crush with a rolling pin.	Ground feeder	Doves, juncos, quail, pheasants, native sparrows
Sugar-coated cereals	—	—	Not appealing to desirable birds; serve in tray or ground feeder during winter storms only when food is scarce

popular treat for backyard birds. You can scatter cereal directly on the ground or in a tray feeder, but birds will gobble it up faster if you make it more palatable by adding tasty peanut butter, peanut oil, or meat drippings to the dry flakes. It's easiest to mix peanut butter and other binders with cereal using your bare hands in a large, deep mixing bowl; the result will be a crumbly mixture that the birds can easily pick up and enjoy.

Many favorite feeder birds appreciate leftover cereal, but so do pigeons, house sparrows, and starlings. If you're trying to discourage these birds from visiting your feeders, offer the cereal mixtures in

Dry cereal makes a great treat for birds— and it's a good way to use up those stale pieces at the bottom of the box.

the chart on the opposite page in small quantities, scattering about a cup at a time among other seed in the feeders. You can also scatter cereal mixes beneath a dense shrub or low-branching conifer to tempt jays, quail, pheasants, and native sparrows. Some of the more traditionally troublesome birds are more reluctant to feed in those places than at open sites.

Choose cereals for birds just as you would for your children or yourself: Those without sugar coating and marshmallows are healthier. Cereals with dried fruit bits or nuts are a special treat that birds will devour with gusto.

CRACKERS

Crackers attract all kinds of birds, including blackbirds, chickadees, crows, doves, jays, juncos, nuthatches, pigeons, titmice, sparrows, starlings, and woodpeckers. You can offer commercial crackers of practically any sort at the feeder. Just break them into small bits that birds can handle. Jays and starlings—and our rodent friends, including squirrels and chipmunks— will also snatch up whole crackers as a real prize. Serve crackers in small amounts because they quickly soak up moisture and become unappealing to all but the hungriest starlings.

For a quick and convenient way to use up bacon grease or beef drippings, crumble saltines into the liquid (but cooled) grease, and stir with a wooden spoon until the coarse cracker crumbs and pieces have soaked up the fat.

DOG FOOD

A 50-pound sack of kibble can go a long way toward keeping your backyard birds well fed. In winter, dry dog food makes an excellent high-protein food for insect-eating birds like wrens and bluebirds. And mockingbirds, starlings, grackles, crows, jays, and other birds who like a little meat in their diet will appreciate an offering of dog chow at any time of year.

Soft dog food is easier for birds to swallow than whole dry pieces, which can get lodged in their throats. To moisten dry kibble, pour just enough hot water over the dog food to give it the consistency of a moist sponge, and set a container of it near a bird-feeding station in your yard. An old lasagna pan or cookie sheet (check thrift shops or yard sales for a bargain-priced selection) makes a good serving container.

When you first start offering dog food, put it out in small amounts—a cup at a time. After you get a feel for how much the birds are eating, you can increase the amount. Dog food that's still in the pan at the end of the day will attract other wildlife to your feeding area: opossums, raccoons, and possibly stray cats, dogs, foxes, or coyotes. If they're not on your list of invited guests, reduce the amount of dog food you offer so that the birds empty the pan during the daytime.

HOT PEPPERS

The small, flat, round seeds from hot peppers (*Capsicum annuum* var. *annuum*) pack a powerfully hot punch to human taste buds, but many birds eat them with impunity. Western sparrows, quail, and other birds that hail from the desert Southwest may sample pepper seeds. Birds of other regions may enjoy them once they become familiar with them.

A plethora of hot peppers are available for home gardens. All do well in well-drained soil in a sunny location, but the plants need a long growing season to produce their best. Any variety will work for using as birdseed.

If you can, allow the plants to stand in your garden for a self-serve buffet. Birds will find the seeds during the fall and winter. Harvesting and cleaning the peppers—which can produce prodigious crops—can be a painful procedure unless you're extremely careful. If you want to clean the fruits to free the seeds, be sure to wear thick rubber gloves to prevent the irritating capsaicin from contacting your skin. Most important, do not rub your eyes or touch unprotected skin once you've begun to work: The burning chemical contaminates your gloves, and the slightest touch can easily transfer the chemical to bare skin.

Quick Reference — LEFTOVERS FOR LUNCH

IF your family's not into leftovers, try feeding the leftovers to the birds. Here are some "people" foods that may find favor with your feathered friends.

FOOD	WHERE TO SERVE	BIRDS ATTRACTED
Cooked corn, on the cob or kernels	Drain any liquid and spread on low tray feeder	Blackbirds, crows, jays, mockingbirds, starlings, woodpeckers
Fruit pies or fruit pastries	Empty suet feeder	Bluebirds, chickadees, mockingbirds, orioles, starlings, titmice
Fruit salad or canned fruit	Drain any liquid and spread on raised tray feeder	House finches, mockingbirds, orioles, starlings, thrashers, Carolina wrens
Lasagna and other pasta dishes with sauce	Directly on ground or on shallow plastic tray low to ground	Crows, jays, magpies, starlings
Meat scraps, any kinds	Empty suet feeder	Chickadees, crows, jays, magpies, starlings, titmice, woodpeckers, Carolina wrens
Quiche	Directly on ground	Chickadees, crows, jays, magpies, starlings, titmice
Sandwiches	Tray feeder or directly on ground	Chickadees, crows, jays, magpies, mockingbirds, robins, starlings, titmice

SALT

Some birds like to eat salt straight, while others prefer just a sprinkling. The easiest way to feed salt is with a long-lasting salt block, which you can get at feed stores for just a few dollars. House finches will be your best customers for salt, but buntings, doves, purple finches, goldfinches, jays, pigeons, pine siskins, house sparrows, and other birds will also partake.

Rain melts salt, causing it to soak into surrounding soil, possibly damaging plants. To avoid tainting your ground and ending up with a large circle of salted "dead zone," settle your salt block on a sturdy waterproof platform with a lip. An upside-down, concave trash can lid, large plastic plant saucer, concrete birdbath bowl, shallow dishpan, or litter tray will work. For a more attractive presentation,

A Need for Grit

WHEN you're feeding the birds, put out some grit along with the seeds. A scattering of gritty coarse sand and small pebbles will appeal to nearly all of your backyard birds. To find out why, just watch a cardinal eating whole dry corn—you'll see that the bird gulps the food down, hard coating and all. It's a wonder birds can digest such tough fare, having no way to chew it first. The secret is their gizzard—a muscular part of their stomachs that breaks down their food into digestible pieces.

Gizzards are designed to work best when they're full of gritty grinding stones, and that's where you can help. Washed, undyed aquarium gravel is an ideal source of larger grit. Builder's sand, the coarse tan variety that you can find at any home-supply store, will serve their need for finer-grade gravel. Crushed eggshells or crushed clam and oyster shells can also provide grit for birds. A little grit goes a long way, so dole it out sparingly, a handful at a time, to keep it from being wasted.

Offer grit on a flat, vegetation-free area of your yard or on top of a large, flat rock near the feeders where birds can easily find it. Choose a raised area so that rain puddles don't submerge the grit. Replenish the supply year-round.

place the salt block on a heavy-duty plastic liner that's held in place with gravel and hidden by a layer of wood chips.

Keep in mind, though, that deer also like salt—so you may want to think twice about giving them another incentive to visit your yard. If deer are a problem, keep the salt block far from any feeders that they can quickly empty. Rabbits, mice, and other animals may also visit a salt block. Nonbird visitors usually visit under the cover of darkness. Shine a strong flashlight on the area or set up a motion-activated light to see who's nibbling on your salt block—or check for teeth marks in the daytime.

SWEET TREATS

Become a regular at the day-old counter of your local doughnut shop, and your chickadees will thank you for it. These high-fat, high-calorie treats are a good source of energy for birds. Chickadees, titmice, mockingbirds, jays, robins, sparrows, starlings, and even bluebirds all enjoy an occasional nibble of doughnut.

Plain doughnuts or doughnut holes, without glaze or powdered sugar coating, are the best choice for feeders. Feed doughnuts in a wire suet basket or other container that allows birds to peck at them but prevents chunks from falling to the ground. You can also stick

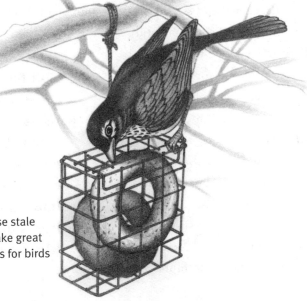

Don't throw out those stale doughnuts. They make great energy-packed treats for birds like this robin.

doughnuts on a spike nail, but be prepared for wholesale thievery by jays, squirrels, and starlings. Jays and starlings may grasp the treat and fly away with as much of it as they can handle.

Cake is another sweet treat that birds enjoy. As with bread, white or light-colored cake pieces and crumbs are the easiest to see and attract birds fastest. Carrot, zucchini, banana, and other moist homemade cakes are ideal for birds, especially if you add a heavy helping of nuts or fruit.

All soft-food eaters dine on cake, including bluebirds, chickadees, jays, mockingbirds, robins, thrushes, titmice, house and native sparrows, and, unfortunately, blackbirds, crows, and starlings.

Cake quickly absorbs moisture and turns moldy fast in wet weather or when spread on the ground. Feed sparingly, or stockpile leftover cake in resealable plastic freezer bags for winter feeding, when birds that eat soft foods, such as bluebirds, robins, and Carolina wrens, may visit feeding stations to seek sustenance.

Birds' grain-based cravings don't stop with doughnuts and cakes, though. Cookies appeal to a variety of birds, too. Birds such as bluebirds, mockingbirds, robins, thrushes, and Carolina wrens that eat mostly soft foods may be tempted by an offering of oatmeal-raisin, chunky peanut butter, or other tasty bird-tailored cookies. Of course, keep in mind that blackbirds, crows, pigeons, house sparrows, and starlings also are fond of soft foods, including cookies.

Crush leftover cookies into coarse crumbs for serving to chickadees, titmice, and soft-food eaters at the feeders. You can also toss a handful of stale cookies from your pantry shelf onto the ground, where house sparrows and other hardy sorts will quickly peck them into bite-size bits.

Soft foods such as cheese, any type of potatoes, salad greens, tomatoes, and vegetables (except corn) do not usually attract desirable birds, but crows and starlings find them interesting.

Freezer Fare

YOUR freezer is a great solution to the potential storage problem you may have with all those soft foods and breads piling up for the birds. Resealable plastic storage bags work great for storage containers. That way, you can see at a glance what's available.

All kinds of food fit into the category of freezer treats: suet, bacon fat, nuts, stale bread and other baked goods, and leftover fruit.

COLLECTING AND PREPARING

Collecting tidbits for your freezer doesn't have to be a time-consuming process. You need only a few plastic storage bags—one for bread, bagels, and other grain-based products; one for old fruit; one for nuts; and one for bacon crumbles and other fat.

Of course, the easiest way to serve freezer treats is to dump the contents into a feeder—but that will also invite a lot of pesky birds. Instead, try combining leftovers into recipes that will attract the birds you treasure most.

For example, try mixing fruit, bread, chopped suet, and peanut butter together into a loaf, and then serving it in a tray feeder. Sure, you'll have to experiment when it comes to figuring out amounts, especially of the binding material, like peanut butter. So start small—you can always add more of something if you need to.

Don't worry about mixing the ingredients thoroughly. Frozen foods clump together, and it's not necessary to have uniform-size small pieces. Just crumble any large lumps so that your mixture holds together better. If your bags have frozen into a solid mass that you can't break up, partially thaw at room temperature or on the defrost setting in your microwave before using.

LESS MESS

Winter is the perfect time to serve freezer treats, when low temperatures slow spoilage and feeder visitors are abundant. Simply stick your treats onto the spike-type feeders you use for corncobs or

Sunflower seed) Niger Millet Flaxseed Berries Grapes Nuts Suet Nectar Bread

orange halves. If you live in a mild-winter area, or if you want to serve your treats at other seasons, offer them in a tray feeder, where birds can snack on any bits that fall away.

One of the big benefits of a freezer is that it makes serving fat-based foods much less messy. In summer, suet blocks and peanut butter can melt in the heat, wasting good food and staining your post or porch with grease. If you serve these foods frozen in the summer, you won't have a mess—and the foods will last longer.

Thirst Quenchers

KEEPING a birdbath filled with water is one of the best things you can do for your backyard birds. Water is vital to birds, not only for drinking but also for cleaning feathers so they can fly properly and stay free from parasites. By providing a fresh source of water in your bird garden, you can attract many species that otherwise would pass you by.

Birds will travel great distances to find water. They drink from any-thing that's available—puddles, streams, ponds, or any container that holds an inch or two of liquid. Some birds, especially those that live in desert regions, meet some of their water needs by eating juicy insects and green plants.

If you really want to put out the water welcome mat, you need to let birds know you have water in the first place. Any device that makes water audible is a prized addition to a bird-attracting yard. Recircu-lating pumps fill the bill, as do fountains in garden pools. Keep in mind that you don't need to create a torrent to attract birds. Their hearing is acute, and they can pick up a ripple or a drip.

In fact, water is so irresistible that the sound of it dripping or burbling or splashing is a guaran-teed draw, no matter where you live. Not only will it bring regular customers to the bath day after day, but it will also tempt migrants in spring and fall.

GENTLE DRIPS

You can create your own dripper by suspending a leaky bucket over the birdbath. Poke a nail into the bucket from the inside to make a single hole in the center. Fill with water and let 'er drip. If you want a splashier sound, poke two to three holes, but keep in mind you'll have to fill the bucket more often.

Commercial dripper devices that attach to your garden hose are widely available. They are a simple piece of copper or other tubing, bent into a curve at the top like the handle of a cane, with a connection for attachment at the other end. These accessories are perfect for a ground-level birdbath or garden pool.

A small fountain in a garden pool creates enough noise to attract birds to the water.

Insect Magnetism

SPRING and summer insects are probably the biggest magnet for birds of all types. These high-protein niblets are everywhere during warm weather, and birds take advantage of the bounty. Soft-bodied insects are also the ideal food for nestlings, which can't crack the seeds in your feeders. When insect life is at its peak, feeder traffic drops off dramatically. Birds don't need to travel to seek sustenance as they do in wintertime—when insects are few and finding wild seeds requires effort. Don't feel discouraged when feeder traffic slackens in late spring. Just bide your time and the birds will return.

FINE MIST

Misting devices, which break up spray into superfine droplets, are a real treat for birds. They exult in the fine spray regularly once they discover it. A mist head that attaches to your hose is a real bargain at about $20. The attachment may tempt bright-colored orioles and tanagers, as well as robins, sparrows, and a host of other songbirds to the delights of the bath. Hummingbirds will also soon be regulars. You can attach the mist head to a branch, post, or other support. Point the spray toward a place where birds can alight to enjoy it. Hummingbirds, of course, need no perch for the pleasure of their bath; an upward-pointing mister is ideal for a hummingbirds-only bathing area.

SPRINKLERS

A good old lawn sprinkler makes a low-tech, low-cost approach to creating water music. Robins, flickers, and hummingbirds are particularly fond of this bath; they will linger beneath the spray for a long time, fluttering their wings as they luxuriate in the gentle water. Birds prefer a sprinkler that waters the same area for a long time rather than an oscillating sprinkler that swings from side to side.

Protein-Packed Wigglers

ROBINS are the number-one nemesis of earthworms, although other birds, including thrushes, may dine on them as well. A subterranean crowd of earthworms will thrive in healthy soil that is high in organic matter. Compost piles are also terrific worm habitats because worms dine on decaying fruit and vegetable matter.

Boost your earthworm population by avoiding toxic lawn chemicals and by layering as much organic matter as you can find on garden beds. Anything that is or was once plant material is fair game, including grass clippings and straw. If worms are in short supply, you can buy worms at a bait shop or from mail-order sources.

FEEDER FUNDAMENTALS

What Feeders Work Best for Your Backyard Birds

IF YOU'VE ALREADY READ through Chapter 2, you know that the fastest way to a bird's heart is through its stomach. Of course, though, if you're going to feed the birds, you need a feeder. And the types of feeders available vary widely. You can choose from hopper and tray feeders, windowsill feeders, suet feeders, nectar feeders—even feederless feeders. And the selection of feeder types available includes designs for serving just about any bird-attracting food you can imagine.

Bird-Feeder Basics

CHOOSING a feeder is a matter of satisfying your needs and those of the birds you hope to attract. The birds that come to your yard will determine the types of food you offer, and the food, in turn, will determine which feeder(s) you use.

When you shop for bird feeders, you'll find that your choices are almost limitless. Here are some hints to help you decide what to buy.

EASE OF USE

The most important factor in choosing a feeder is how easy it is to use—for both you and the birds.

Test out the feeder in the store. Is the feeder easy to open to pour in seed? Remember that it won't be sitting on a convenient shelf when you refill—it will probably be swinging from a hanger or atop a post, and you'll be opening the feeder with one hand while you hold the container of fresh seed in the other. If you can do the imaginary filling job without frustration, take the feeder home with you. If it's tricky to handle in the store, it will likely be even more frustrating in your backyard on a cold, snowy day when you're wearing a pair of heavy gloves or mittens.

You'll also want a feeder that holds a reasonable amount of seed (at least a quart). If you're just getting started, look for a feeder that displays seed in full view because birds are attracted by the sight of food as well as by the sight of other birds eating. An open tray is great for starters.

Make sure your feeder has plenty of room for birds to eat without protrusions or decorations getting in the way. Birds also like a feeder with a raised ledge or perch that they can grasp while dining.

Check whether you can take the feeder apart to clean it. Are there corners and crannies that are hard to reach? If so, you can be sure that seed will end up stuck there, and old seed can mold and cause birds to get sick.

Size of Feeders

When birds come to a feeder, they want food, and they want it fast. At least one of your feeders should be a large one that holds plenty of seed and plenty of birds. Otherwise, you'll be spending an inordinate amount of time trekking to the feeder to refill.

A large tray feeder that's big enough for at least a dozen birds to eat at once is a good starting point. Supplement that with hopper- and tube-type feeders. Domed feeders

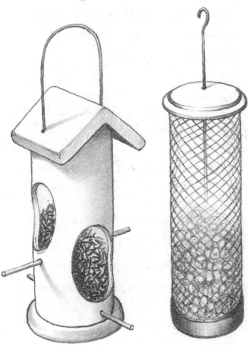

You can buy feeders for specific foods, such as niger *(left)* and nuts *(right)*.

are great for small birds like chick-adees. Feeders inside wire cages give small birds a place to eat in peace without competition from starlings or other larger birds.

Once you have one or two large feeders, you can add as many small ones as you like. Clear plastic feeders, for example, that attach to a window with suction cups are nice because they bring the birds right up to your eye level.

FEEDER QUALITY

Feeder prices vary dramatically from one supplier to another. Homemade feeders are the least costly, whether you make them yourself from materials you have on hand or buy them at nearby nature centers or other outlets for local craftspeople. Feeders of unusual, complicated design are much more expensive. In between, you'll find dozens of models priced affordably.

Shoddy feeders are no bargain. They'll fall apart when it's least convenient—usually just after you've filled them with the last of your seed supply. And squirrels will take advantage of lightweight and poorly constructed feeders by chewing through them with amazing speed or by dropping them to the ground to spill out the contents. Examine the feeder before you buy, and look for signs of good quality (see "Quality Matters" below).

Quality Matters

SHELLING out a few extra dollars for a well-made feeder is well worth it. Look for a feeder with these features:

- Solid wood, not plywood
- Nails or screws, not staples, at joints
- Sturdy screened bottoms in tray feeders (for drainage in wet weather and improved air circulation to prevent mold formation)

- Strong attachments for hangers
- Metal reinforcement around feeder holes to keep pesky squirrels from chewing their way to the seed inside

Types of Feeders

FEEDER design hasn't changed drastically over the last few decades, simply because the styles that worked well years ago still work today. Most seed feeders are simple constructions of wood, metal, or plastic that are built to last for years. Those with hoppers that dole out seed automatically are designed to hold a good quantity so that you don't have to refill frequently. Other types of feeders are tailor-made for offering birds special treats other than the staple seeds.

HOPPER FEEDERS

Hopper feeders are feeders with built-in seed storage. These handy devices dole out seed as quickly as it disappears from the surrounding tray so that you don't have to bother with daily refills. The seed is stored in a plastic or glass enclosure that's covered to protect it from rain and snow; a slit or other opening at the bottom allows the stored seed to run out and fill the tray as your guests empty it out.

Not only do hopper feeders save you time, they also guarantee that fresh seed is available to birds even when you aren't around to refill. Many birds, including chickadees, nuthatches, titmice, cardinals, jays, and woodpeckers, eat eagerly at a hopper feeder.

You can choose from many designs of hopper feeders on the market. You can buy lightweight, clear plastic models or huge, heavy metal or wood constructions that hold up to 10 pounds of seed—and several styles in between. Fill the feeder with whatever seeds your birds like best: millet, sunflower, or a mix.

You can easily transform plastic soda bottles into bird feeders. Using a sharp-bladed kitchen knife, slice the bottom off of a 2-liter soda bottle. Nail two or three of these plastic cups to a board and fill them with raisins, chopped apples, ground suet, and other treats.

Because hopper feeders are more complicated in structure than simple tray feeders, they are also more expensive. Expect to pay from $30 to $75 for a well-made hopper feeder. These feeders are worth the initial investment, though, because you and your bird friends will be using them for years.

Limited feeding space is the only drawback of hopper feeders. The storage area often takes up most of the space, leaving only a narrow ledge for birds to eat from. They can't accommodate as many birds at one sitting as an open tray feeder. Some designs compensate for this by attaching a wider tray area beneath the hopper.

A hopper feeder's built-in storage guarantees that birds will have fresh seed.

MESH BAG FEEDERS

Mesh bags are one of the easiest and most convenient feeders, both for you to make and hang and for birds to visit and feed from. Mesh bags (such as plastic mesh bags used to hold onions and other produce at the supermarket) make great impromptu feeders when the need arises. You can fill them with suet, nutmeats, peanuts, sunflower seed, raisins, or anything else that won't fall out between the holes in the mesh. And it's easy for birds to slip their beaks between the strands and pick out the delicacies you serve them.

You can also buy commercial prefilled mesh bags, which are convenient because you don't have to fill them or tie them shut—just hang them on a nail or hook and they're ready for customers. Although these bags are sold as disposables, you can reuse them several times. (If you reuse them, you'll need to cut an opening at the top of the bag so you can refill it.) Their mesh is finer than the mesh bags for produce, so you can fill them with a wider variety of smaller food items.

NECTAR FEEDERS

Easy cleaning is the main priority when you shop for a nectar feeder. Sugar water can mold quickly, so you'll need to swab out the feeder before every refill. Make sure the feeder model you like comes apart easily and allows you to get into all those nooks and crannies.

Horizontally oriented feeders, with the drinking holes above the solution, are available in very easy-to-clean models that separate into halves that are as simple to wash as salad plates. Vertically oriented feeders, the most commonly available, are more difficult to clean because only the cap comes off. Buy yourself a bottle brush to make the job quick and easy. (Make sure the feeder isn't opaque; if it is, you won't be able to tell when the sugar water is getting low.)

If this is your first nectar feeder, choose one with lots of red plastic to grab the attention of passing hummingbirds. Install all first-time feeders in an open area, where birds can easily see them. Once you have regulars at the feeder, you can move it to another part of the garden.

SUET FEEDERS

Simple wire cages are an excellent way to serve suet. You can either slide in a preformed commercial block, or stuff the cage yourself with chunks of fat from the butcher. The sturdy grid of wire protects the suet from being carried off whole by other feeder visitors, especially nocturnal prowlers like cats and coons. Suet cages are quite inexpensive to buy—they're about $5 a pop.

Mesh Suet Feeders

BECAUSE suet is so popular, you might want to save those mesh onion and potato bags year-round so you can hang lots of suet feeders during the months of peak demand. You can stuff these strong plastic mesh bags with as much or as little suet or beef scraps as you like. Hook the bags onto a nail or other hanger, or hang them from a length of string attached to the branches of shrubs or trees.

Cat-food and tuna cans, as well as containers from yogurt, cottage cheese, and sour cream, can also be recycled into fat feeders. Wash the containers, melt suet, or collect bacon grease or other meat drippings, cool, and pour into the containers. Once the fat solidifies, you'll have a delectable bird treat.

TRAY FEEDERS

A simple, shallow tray has great bird appeal. The seed is in plain view, so it attracts visitors quickly to a new feeding station. The feeder accommodates many birds at a time, thanks to its ledges and wide-open tray. There's plenty of room for all birds, even when aggressive types visit, because of the large feeding area. And the birds can fly in and out freely, plus have a clear view in all directions.

Most tray feeders (also known as platform feeders) are made from wood or plastic, although a clay saucer or even a plastic cafeteria tray can adequately serve the same purpose. As with any other bird

Bird Watching

THE closer you get to a bird, the more fun it is to watch. But because birds are naturally wary creatures, you're not likely to get a glimpse of interesting behaviors as long as the birds are aware of your presence. A portable semi-permanent bird blind that keeps you hidden while you watch is easier to make than you might think, depending on what kind of habitat you want to watch birds in and what kind of materials you have handy.

For watching feeder birds, the windows of your house make the perfect vantage point as long as you avoid drawing attention to your presence with vigorous or sudden movements. For the best view, position your feeders as close to the windows as you can. Windowsill feeders are a wonderful choice because they bring the birds near enough to let you see every detail. You could also install inexpensive stick-on film that turns the window into a one-way mirror, from which you can see out clearly but the birds outside see only a reflection of themselves.

A good-quality wooden tray feeder has screws—not staples—at the joints.

feeder that will get heavy use, inspect before you buy to look for signs of solid construction.

Before buying a wood feeder, check to make sure it has screws or nails, not staples, at the joints, and that it's made of solid wood, not plywood or pressed fiberboard. A plastic feeder should be made of material that includes an ultraviolet inhibitor so that it doesn't degrade quickly in sunlight. Also check for a heavy, solid feel; a flimsy feeder won't last for long.

All tray feeders should have drainage so that rainwater doesn't puddle in the seed. Many wood feeders have a stiff screened bottom that helps the seed drain quickly and increases circulation to help stave off mold. Other wood models, and most plastic feeders, have drain holes drilled in the bottom to accomplish the same objectives.

Nearly all birds will accept a tray feeder. Chickadees, finches, grosbeaks, jays, and titmice will be your best customers right from the start, followed soon after by buntings, cardinals, nuthatches—and all other seed-eating birds. The only birds reluctant to use a tray feeder mounted on a post are ground-feeding birds. A very low tray on stumpy legs will accommodate these birds, which include native sparrows, quail, towhees, and doves. You can put any kind of seed in a tray except for tiny niger, lettuce, and grass seeds, which are apt to blow away or get wasted (put these in a tube feeder instead). Tray feeders are also good places to put doughnuts, bread crumbs, and fruit.

TUBE FEEDERS

If you consider yourself on the frugal side of things, then tube feeders are for you. Tube feeders save you money because they conserve seed; birds pull out just a seed or two at a time, so little is wasted to spills or messy eaters.

Tube feeders are easy to use, too. Slide up the lid, pour in the seeds, and the feeder is stocked for as long as a few weeks, depending on the size of your feeder and the traffic it gets.

Tube feeders are also the only practical way to offer tiny niger seed, which is easily blown out of other feeders. In addition, tube feeders are used only by small birds, including finches, redpolls, and pine siskins. Starlings and other perching birds can't get a grip on the short perches.

Make sure you read the label to find out what kind of seed your tube feeder was designed for. The size of the hole determines whether you have a feeder that should be filled with niger, birdseed mix, or sunflower seeds.

Just keep in mind that not all tube feeders are created equal. You

Ground Feeding

SOME birds, such as doves, juncos, sparrows, and towhees, prefer their food as close to the ground as possible. To help them out, you can purchase a low-level tray feeder (or you can make one yourself). A large rock with a concave surface also makes an ideal bird feeder for ground-feeding birds.

Pouring seed or other food directly on the ground can lead to problems for birds because the food may quickly turn moldy in wet weather. If birds do eat moldy food, they may suffer health problems such as aspergillosis, a serious fungal infection that can quickly spread through birds feeding at spoiled grain. Spreading seed directly on the ground will also encourage mice and other rodents to visit.

You can still feed birds on the ground if you feed small amounts at a time, so the seed doesn't accumulate and spoil (or attract rodents), and remove any seed that gets wet.

might want to invest a few extra dollars in the more expensive models (such as those made by Duncraft). The tube itself is sturdier, the feeding holes are designed better so there's less spillage of seeds as birds eat, and the heavier metal used on top and bottom makes the feeder more stable. (Lightweight plastic models may swing easily in the wind, scattering seed on the ground.)

WINDOWSILL FEEDERS

You can mount a simple shallow tray feeder on the outside of a window, mounting it like a window box (but higher and closer to the pane). You can use wooden or metal brackets that attach below or on the sill. To fill the feeder, simply open the window and pour seeds into the tray.

Feeders that attach to your window with suction cups are also a great invention. Clear plastic stick-on feeders that are about the size of caged-bird feeding cups are perfect for small birds such as chickadees, goldfinches, nuthatches, and titmice.

FEEDERLESS FEEDERS

In addition to buying an actual product to house bird food, you can buy something known as a feederless feeder: a compressed block of food that makes its own feeder. At about 8 inches square, the blocks are a bit smaller than a salt block—and as an added benefit, they last a long time.

You can buy seed blocks made from sunflower, millet, and other favored seeds, or from a combination of corn, sunflower, and peanuts. Both mixtures appeal to birds as well as to squirrels, chipmunks, and other feeder visitors. Simply set the block on the ground, and it's ready to eat.

Filling feeders doesn't get any easier than with a tray feeder.

Compressed cornmeal, formed into a hard-packed cylinder for gnawing or pecking, is also available as a feederless feeder. The cylinder pushes onto a metal rod in a similar fashion to a corncob feeder. Although they cost more than corncobs, the cylinders are waste-free because all parts of them are edible and longer-lasting, so you won't have to refill as often. They are also more difficult for pesky squirrels to remove from the spike than a corncob, which means they won't disappear after a day or two. They're good for offering on decks or balconies.

Seed bells—birdseed mix packed into a molded bell shape—are still around, as well. The bell accommodates only a single customer or two and is accessible to any clinging bird—chickadees, finches, nuthatches, titmice, and woodpeckers are the usual customers. Once the bell begins to acquire an irregular shape after weeks of nibbling, it may also be visited by less agile birds such as jays, mockingbirds, and starlings.

Feeder Covers

ALTHOUGH an open, uncovered feeder gives you a great view of the birds that come to visit, an uncovered feeder also gives soaring hawks a fine look at a potential next meal. And it exposes the seed—and the birds—to rain, snow, and wind. Uncovered feeders also give squirrels and other seed hogs easy access to the seed you put out for your feathered friends.

You can make your own tray feeder cover by a screwing a piece of plywood to the rear corners of the tray with wing nuts. Or, try stapling branches of spruce and hemlock to the edge of the tray feeder that faces the wind.

To keep pests from stealing your birds' food, cover your feeder with a wire-grid feeder cover. These covers snap into place over tray feeders, keeping out pests but allowing birds to still reach the food with their beaks. Some wire-grid feeder covers even have holes in them that are large enough to keep out pests but small enough to allow small birds to fit between them, where they can dine in peace.

HAND-FEEDING

If patience is one of your virtues, then you'll have an advantage when it comes to hand-feeding birds. Winter is the best season to tame birds because hunger is a big incentive for birds to get over their natural fear of humans. The morning after a big snow- or ice storm, when food sources are at a premium, you can tame birds in 20 minutes or less just by holding out a heaping handful of food.

Birds are difficult to hand-tame in late spring and summer, though, because natural food is abundant. You can train feeder birds to eat out of your hand during these seasons by becoming a regular presence near the feeder. Time your visits for early morning, when birds are hungriest after a night without food.

Start by emptying all feeders except a basic open tray model. Fill that feeder, than pull up a lawn chair near the feeder, about 3 feet away. Your guests, which probably headed for the hills when you arrived, should return in about a half-hour. Remain sitting quietly while they feed for another half-hour.

Repeat this process the next day, but this time position your chair directly beside the feeder. The third day, rest your hand in the feeder, with a tempting handful of nuts or sunflower seeds in your palm. Don't worry if birds eat the seeds around your hand but not those in it; just stay still and non-threatening.

The fourth day, empty the feeder and repeat the offering on your palm. You should get at least one taker—generally a chickadee or titmouse.

Continue sitting on the chair for another day or two, until birds freely visit your hand. Then try standing at the feeder. Once a few friendly birds accept you as a new walking feeder, they may alight on your shoulder to ask for feed as you stroll the yard.

You'll find it easy to gain the confidence of chickadees, nuthatches, downy woodpeckers, and titmice. Simply tempt them with unsalted raw peanuts, walnuts, pecans, or sunflower seeds.

Feeder Fundamentals

Q Although my own cat is an indoors-only feline, my neighbor lets her cat out on a regular basis—and more than once I've caught him stalking the birds at my feeders. What can I do to protect the birds from this cat?

A Protecting birds from a neighborhood feline is a dilemma. The best thing to do is to chase kitty away whenever you see him in or near your yard. However, cats aren't stupid, and the attraction of birds is so great that he'll probably return as soon as you go away. A dog is really your best defense against cats. Dogs rarely chase birds, because they're usually unsuccessful at catching them; dogs are also easier to train to stay away from the feeding station.

Q Last year, I had a water feature installed in my backyard. Although I think it looks great, I don't see very many birds taking advantage of it. Do you have any suggestions for how I can make this pretty pool more inviting for the birds?

A In a backyard water feature, birds need a secure place to perch while drinking, or access to shallow water for bathing. You might want to lay rocks into one end of the pool so that their surfaces are just below water level, with part of the rock above the water. This will give birds a place to stand for drinking. Leave spaces between some of the rocks around the rim of the pool to provide a sheltered nook where birds can get a drink or wet a feather. You might also place a variety of potted aquatic plants close to the edge of the pool, in the water, so that the surface of their containers extends to or very near the rim of the pool.

Feeder Mounts

THESE days, your choices for mounting feeders aren't limited to a tree branch or a wooden post that you've sunk into the ground. The introduction of the black metal shepherd's crook offers you a mount that's easy to install and looks good in the garden.

Shepherd's crooks come in many varieties to suit your yard, your feeders, and your bird population. You can find single-armed models to hold a lone nectar feeder, tube feeder, or seed feeder. Double-armed designs will easily secure a pair of feeders. There are even crooks with multiple arms at the top to attach several feeders.

Arts and crafts shows are great places to pick up interesting feeder mounts, as blacksmithing is making a comeback. Antique shops and architectural salvage stores are good places to look for feeder mounts that function as garden ornaments.

Keep in mind, though, that while shepherd's crooks are strong, they can sometimes tip with the weight of their customers. A wood post's solid heft supports tray feeders securely, and its brawn is well matched to the proportions of most seed feeders. Wood posts also have a natural look that blends in with plantings.

TASTEFUL CHOICES

Feeders are a focal point in the garden, drawing your eye as much as any carefully chosen garden ornament. Before you begin adding bird feeders willy-nilly, consider the overall look of your installations. Select the design of feeder mountings just as you would with a piece of statuary. For tasteful good looks, keep it simple, and keep the following design concepts in mind.

■ **Match proportions.** Large feeders hanging from skinny poles or chains jar the eye because of disproportion. Match your feeders to their mounts according to their size and weight.

feeders

Tubes Windowsills Hangers Baffles Birdbaths

■ **Employ repetition.** Use similar mounts, or those with complementary features, rather than mixing and matching different styles. Keep colors similar, too—avoid mixing black and white poles, for example.

■ **Think straight and solid.** For the most unobtrusive arrangement, choose hangers and stands with straight lines and solid shafts, such as metal poles, long steel hooks, or wooden posts. A dozen feeders dangling from chains can make your backyard look rather junky.

■ **Practice simplicity.** It's easy to purchase and install shepherd's crook iron hangers, but a forest of black stands can have the same effect as a gathering of pink flamingos. So don't go overboard.

■ **Go easy on the curves.** Curved lines call for attention. So keep them to a minimum, or arrange them in a coherent way so that the eye travels naturally from one to the other rather than jumping about. Three curving iron hooks look better stacked in a vertical arrangement on the same side of a tall post than they do staggered at varying heights and positions around the post.

HANGER HINTS

Most feeders are sold with a handle or hook on top for hanging. Take a look at this attachment before you buy to make sure it is sturdy and strongly attached with screws or bolts rather than staples. If a wood feeder is cracked at the

Avoiding Waste

WHEN purchasing your hanging equipment, go easy on the chain—swinging feeders waste seed. Niger, nectar, and small seeds can spill out easily with every sway of the feeder. Choose hooks and hangers that will keep your feeders as stable as possible. The longer the chain or series of hooks, the more wildly the feeder will swing in strong winds or under the weight of arriving and departing customers.

point of attachment, pass it up. Look for one with a handle or hook that will hold up to heavy wear.

Also determine whether the feeder hanger will get in the way of refilling the feeder. If you have to jiggle the lid of the feeder to open it because of an intrusive handle, re-filling will be a chore. Look for tube feeders with lids that slide up the bail of the handle, instead of those that have to be completely re-moved and replaced after filling (and thus creating an opportunity for misplaced lids).

When selecting hooks and chains (which you can find in garden centers and bird supply shops), keep stability in mind. Al-though birds are featherweights, seed adds pounds to the weight of the feeder, and squirrels can drop with force from nearby trees. Choose S-hooks that will support the weight of the birds, chain, feeder, and seed.

Baffles

SQUIRRELS, raccoons, and similar animals may be welcome guests in your yard, but most birders prefer that these critters stick to their own feeders and leave the bird feeders alone. Not only do they tend to clean out a bird feeder in a hurry, but a resident squirrel will also deter most birds from vis-iting the feeder while it dines. For reasons unclear to us humans, squirrels will almost always go for the bird feeders first. That's where baffles come in—they help put a barrier between seeds and squirrels.

WHAT IS A BAFFLE?

Baffles are metal or plastic guards that stand between the feeder and the tree or post so that climbing animals can't mount a sneak attack on the food. Keep in mind that squirrels are determined creatures, and they may eventually overcome a baffle. They may figure out an alternative approach route and leap directly to the feeder. At best, a baffle will keep squirrels thwarted all season long; at least, it will slow them down a bit.

PROTECTING FEEDERS

If your feeder is mounted on a post, first be sure that squirrels can't reach it by leaping onto it from a tree or roof. Then install a metal cone-shaped or tubular baffle below the feeder. Tubular baffles must be about 14 inches long to deter squirrels and 24 inches long to keep out raccoons. You can make your own baffle from a section of pipe, chosen to fit the diameter of your post, or you can purchase a commercial baffle for easy installation. A section of plastic PVC pipe slipped over the post will deter squirrels for a little while, although they may eventually gnaw through it. Spray-paint the pipe dark green or black to make it less obtrusive in the landscape. Commercial baffles (available at garden and bird centers and home-supply shops) are widely available for both tubular metal posts and thicker wood posts; for a well-made design that will last for years, expect to pay between $15 and $30.

To protect hanging feeders, slip a metal or plastic baffle between the feeder and its hanging hook. This baffle prevents access by tipping as the squirrel climbs onto it, sending the animal sliding off the side or scurrying back where it came from. The slick plastic or metal also prevents the squirrel's feet from getting a secure grip. If you have a choice, go for a metal baffle. Remember that a determined squirrel will gnaw its way through a plastic device. No matter what type of feeder guard you install, keep an eye out—the most persistent and pesky of squirrels may eventually figure out a way around even the most well-designed feeder guard.

Some newer models of feeders now come equipped with weight-activated baffles. When a squirrel—or even a large, feeder-hogging pigeon—puts its weight on the perch bar, the pressure pulls down a solid metal wall between the unwanted guest and the food within the feeder. You can even adjust the balance to give only lightweight songbirds access to the seeds—and keep everyone else out. Sturdy steel construction adds heft and cost to these bird-food fortresses, but you can recover the price rather quickly in savings on seeds.

Feeder Placement

THE life and color birds bring to the view outside the window is well worth the small investment in birdseed and other goodies. That's why the best place for your feeders is where you can see them. There's no point placing feeders far away from the house unless you want to attract shier birds that tend to stay back, or you need more than one feeding station in order to accommodate a crowd.

A FINE VIEW

When you place your feeders near a window in your house, you'll have a fine view of bird activity with or without binoculars. Plan the position for your feeders according to how you spend your time in the house. If you wash dishes by hand, a feeder outside the window over the sink is in a perfect place. If your family gathers around the kitchen table for breakfast each morning, outside a window near the table is another excellent site. A multifeeder setup outside a family room window is a possibility, as well. Just make sure you can clearly see the feeders from a sitting position and that comfortable chairs are available so that everyone can view the show.

Crashing Birds

PUTTING a feeder far away from your house actually increases the possibility of birds crashing into your windows. Birds are apt to fly up in a panic from a feeder many times a day when danger threatens—such as when a hawk flies overhead. The birds dash off in all directions, flying at top speed to get to cover. When a bird is scared and moving fast, the reflections of trees and shrubs in window glass may seem to offer sanctuary.

If your feeder is very close to your window—within 5 feet or so—birds are unlikely to get up enough speed to seriously hurt themselves if they should collide with it.

PROVIDE SHELTER

It will take you longer to lure birds to a feeder in the middle of a wide, bare lawn than to a feeder that is in a well-shrubbed area. Birds feel safer if there is cover near the feeder into which they can quickly retreat should danger threaten. Visiting a feeder in the middle of a lawn is asking for trouble, from a bird's point of view.

A group of shrubs or a single conifer can provide enough shelter to make birds feel more comfortable. Flowerbeds, shade trees, veg-

A feeder hung amidst cover, such as shade trees, will make birds feel safe.

etable gardens, ornamental grasses, and berry patches all contribute to a bird's sense of safety.

FEEDERS HIGH AND LOW

Birds such as chickadees and woodpeckers that spend most of their time in the trees are accustomed to eating at higher levels than birds such as towhees and sparrows that usually skulk about at ground level. That's why you'll want to place your feeders accordingly.

Birds will adapt to feeders at unaccustomed heights if they are hungry enough. But your aim is to attract birds not only during winter blizzards, when the snow covers everything in sight. You also want to tempt birds to your feeders even when natural food is competing for their attention. Putting up both high and low feeders is an important way to make birds feel at home.

PROPER PROTECTION

Keeping warm and dry is a primary concern of birds because calories burned to stay cozy mean less energy to fuel other body functions. You'll want to put your feeder in a place protected from chilling fall and winter winds, and out of the line of driving rain and snow. Seasonal wind direction varies in different parts of the country, but in general, cold air tends to move from the north or northwest.

Block the path of prevailing winds with existing shrubs and trees or with newly planted windbreaks. Evergreens are best for the job because their dense foliage is effective in winter. You can also erect trellises of vines to cut the wind.

EASY FILLING

Another reason to place feeders near the house is so that you don't have far to go to refill—which can be every morning during peak season. Keep in mind where the door of your house and the seed storage area are when you choose a feeder location. A short walk in summer may be an arctic trek come December.

If you live in an area of particularly bad winters, consider a convenient windowsill-mounted feeder, which will allow you to refill from inside the house.

Keeping the Peace

A well-used feeding station can strain relations with your neighbors if you're attracting hordes of birds to your yard, or if your feeder is near a property line. To keep the peace:

■ Alter your feeder offerings to discourage blackbirds or other birds that are becoming a nuisance. Large gray-striped sunflower seeds are usually less appealing to flocking birds.

■ Switch to tube feeders if starlings or blackbirds have become a pain.

■ Limit highly visible foods such as bread, baked goods, and larger fruits to contained feeders instead of scattering it on the ground where it might look like debris from a distance.

■ Keep the feeder area looking tidy by frequently freshening the mulch beneath the feeders and removing the hulls if needed.

feeders

Hoppers Mesh bags Trays Tubes Windowsills Hangers Baffles Birdbaths

Good Housekeeping

WHEN it comes to bird feeders, good housekeeping is a must. Because a feeding station is an unnatural situation (so many birds crowded into a small space, all eating from the same tray), illnesses can spread like wildfire. Basic cleanliness will keep your birds healthy and prevent disease from spreading through the flock you've invited to your yard.

KEEPING THINGS FRESH

To make sure problems don't start at your feeders, keep your seed and nectar fresh. Damp or wet birdseed can sprout *Aspergillus* mold, which can infect birds when the fungus releases its spores into the air. As sick birds huddle at the feeders, their droppings contaminate the seed and spread the disease to other birds.

In wet weather, refill your feeders sparingly so that the seed is consumed before it can absorb moisture. Refilling the feeders more frequently is better than wasting money on wet seed. To keep tiny niger seed fresh and dry in tube feeders, add a few handfuls of uncooked rice to the seed when you fill the feeder.

If seed gets wet, scoop it out of the feeders and dispose of it. Let the feeder dry before you refill it. Cover the area beneath your feeders with a 2-inch layer of bark chips or shredded mulch. When shells reach the messy stage, turn over the mulch to hide them and add a new topping of mulch. Or keep the area bare and rake up the shells periodically.

KEEPING THINGS CLEAN

How often you clean your feeders depends on how much bird traffic you get and on the weather. Remove spoiled seed and empty hulls whenever they accumulate; a garden hose works great to spray feeders clean fast and to wash out tube feeders, plastic suction-cup window feeders (take them down first), and other feeders with nooks and crannies that are hard to reach with a brush. Allow the feeders to dry thoroughly before you refill them, or the moisture may cause the seed to turn moldy.

Once each season, swab down your feeders with a 10 percent bleach solution (9 parts water to 1 part bleach). Don a pair of rubber gloves and, using a stiff brush, scrub the surfaces, roofs, and sides of tray feeders and the feeding shelves and perches of other feeders, which are likely spots for germs to accumulate. Again, allow the feeders to dry before you refill them with seed.

Specially designed brushes that have angled tips, long wire handles, or other improvements to make feeder cleaning easier may be worth investing in, especially since most of them cost just a few dollars. Take a look at each gadget's size and shape before you buy it to decide whether you'll actually use it enough to warrant adding it to your collection.

Of course, once you begin cleaning your feeders, you'll develop an appreciation for the ones that are easy to clean!

Nectar Feeders

THE best way to save time cleaning a nectar feeder is to buy a well-designed feeder in the first place. Since you'll most likely be cleaning and refilling the feeder every few days for months on end, you'll save yourself a lot of frustration by choosing a product that is fast and simple to disassemble, with unobstructed access to all parts of the feeder.

Check the accessories aisle of a local bird-supply store or a specialty catalog like those listed on page 202 for brushes that will make cleaning your feeder easier. At a cost of only a few dollars, these small, flexible brushes are a bargain because they'll save you hours of time over the nectar season. Regular bottle brushes, available in any discount store and many supermarkets, work well for cleaning the main reservoir of nectar feeders. Pipe cleaners are also handy for snaking grime out of the feeding holes of nectar feeders. If you use plastic snap-on devices to deter bees at the feeder holes, use an old toothbrush for a quick cleanup across their grids.

feeders

Hoppers Mesh bags Trays Tubes Windowsills Hangers Baffles Birdbaths

Feeder Maintenance

THE wear and tear of birds, squirrels, and weather takes its toll on feeders. Hooks may pull free, side boards may split, corners may come unglued. Luckily, a little timely repair will usually save the day and give your feeder more years of useful life.

BASIC FEEDER REPAIRS

Even if you're not a natural-born handyperson, you can still manage a number of basic feeder repairs. All you need are a few tools of the trade that are useful for making quick feeder fixes.

A can of wood putty is great for filling cracks and holes where a hook has pulled free. A **putty knife's** flat metal blade is useful for digging putty out of the can and applying it where holes and cracks need filling.

Screw-in eye hooks work great when a feeder will no longer hang from its original hook, usually because the wood has rotted around the old screw. **Wire coat hangers** are flexible enough to bend into shape, yet strong enough to support a new feeder. They're a great source of new hooks and hanging material.

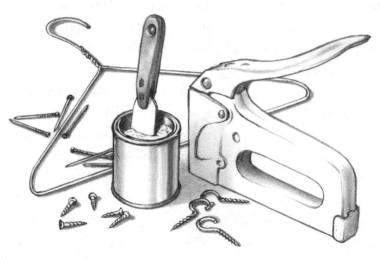

A few basic tools are all you need to breathe new life into a worn feeder.

You can use **L-shaped metal hinges** to reinforce corners that have pulled apart on metal feeders. Buy the largest size that will fit your edges, and screw them on with rustproof screws.

An **assortment of screws and nails** are handy to have around when you need to do quick repairs. You can buy a prepackaged assortment, or assemble your own at a hardware store that sells loose nails and screws by weight. Make sure

you get weatherproof hardware that won't rust during wet weather.

A **heavy-duty staple gun** is key because you can do a lot with staples—and fast. You can use staples to rejoin corners that have pulled apart, attach a new side ledge, or hang a mesh bag of suet from a post. Keep in mind, though, that staples aren't a permanent fix for feeder repairs; eventually, it's best to replace them with nails.

REPLACING GLASS

A broken hopper isn't the end of the line for a feeder, as long as the rest of it is in decent shape. Carefully remove the broken glass, and measure it exactly. Then check the yellow pages of your telephone book to find a business that cuts glass to size. Check whether the glass slides within a channel; if it does, take a piece of the original glass along when you go to order the glass so that they can match the thickness. Consider replacing the glass of a hopper feeder with clear, heavy-duty rigid plastic, which won't pose the danger of broken glass in case of another accident.

TOOLS OF THE TRADE
at a glance

You need only these tools to make simple feeder repairs:
- Wood putty and putty knife
- Screw-in eye hooks
- Wire coat hangers
- L-shaped metal hinges
- Screws and nails
- Staple gun

feeders

Windowsills Hangers Baffles Birdbaths

Pests at the Feeder

BIRDS and animals can easily become nuisances at your feeders, thanks to the abundance of delicious food there for the taking. Changing the menu to foods they find less appealing and changing the feeders to models they can't use are the best alternatives.

OUTWITTING SQUIRRELS

To put it bluntly, squirrels aren't stupid. They can figure out how to raid almost any bird feeder, including those sold as squirrel-proof. Combine their smarts with agility and leaping ability, and you have a creature that's hard to foil at the feeder.

Squirrels can consume enormous amounts of birdseed and other feeder treats. Although they're willing to eat peaceably beside birds, their presence is enough to keep away most of the regulars. And once a squirrel arrives, it's there for the long haul. It sits quietly in the feeder, snacking through seeds for an hour or more before it's had enough and moves on—only to make way for the next squirrel in line. If squirrels are raiding too many of your feeders too often, try some of these tactics to save your birdseed for the birds.

■ Mount your feeder on a smooth metal pole surrounded by a stationary or sliding metal baffle.

If You Can't Beat 'Em . . .

IF you give squirrels their own feeding setup, they may leave your bird feeders alone (at least for a while). Squirrels will eagerly eat cracked corn from a tray feeder, or you can make a corn feeder with a whole cob of corn. Simply hammer a large nail through a 4-inch-square piece of 2 × 4 board, and push a whole cob of corn onto the nail. Then fasten on a second piece of board for a backboard that you can mount onto a pole or tree. Forcing the squirrels to nibble the corn off the cob helps slow down their consumption.

■ Put a dome-shaped plastic baffle over a hanging feeder.

■ Make sure your feeders are more than a squirrel's-leap away from any overhanging tree branches, eaves, or other launching areas.

■ Try a tube feeder within a metal cage. The cage keeps squirrels out while the space between the bars allows finches, chickadees, and other small birds to pass in and out.

■ Remove the bottom spill tray from hanging feeders, which will make it harder for squirrels to hang on.

■ Get a dog. A dog will definitely make squirrels think twice about treating your yard as their own private nature preserve.

■ Buy seed treated with hot pepper extract. It really does work, although be prepared to pay more than you would for untreated seed.

FEATHERED PESTS

Feathered pests fall into two categories: bullies and hordes. Crows, jays, mockingbirds, and ravens are the bullies. They can wreak havoc with the gentle daily life of a feeding station by chasing away less aggressive birds with raucous calls or threatening dashes. Mockingbirds can be especially irritating because, unlike the other bullies, they don't leave the feeder when they're through eating. They stick around the feeder area, making life miserable for any other bird that dares to approach. The solution to bully birds is to add more feeders, especially models that prevent them from patronizing the feeder. In the case of a territorial mockingbird, you can empty the feeders altogether until the bird moves on, or you can set up other feeders at a location separated by a large visual barrier, such as a high fence or your house.

Bird pests that arrive in hordes are troublesome because they use up most of the feeder space as well as gobble much of the food. One starling at a time is not a problem; when a dozen of them descend on your suet feeders, there's no room for a wren or a nuthatch to get a bite. Blackbirds flock in fall and winter, arriving in multitudes. Feeders with protective wire grids or cages, or with weight-sensitive perches, are highly effective at keeping at least some of your feeders free for the use of smaller birds. You might also try adding more feeders or offering cracked corn, an excellent decoy food for blackbirds, well away from other feeders.

DEER

Bambi can be a real nuisance at the feeding station, causing just as much damage as he and his friends and family do in the garden. Instead of nibbling a mere handful of seeds over the course of the day, deer can vacuum your feeders to bare wood in just one short visit. And because bird-feeder design doesn't accommodate large animals, deer can damage the feeders as well as eat you out of 6 months' supply of birdseed.

If deer are only occasional visitors to your yard or if you enjoy watching them, you may want to set up a feeding station just for them. Of course, there's no way to put up a no-trespassing sign at other feeders. But by offering a bounty of their favorite foods, you may be able to keep them confined to an area apart from more fragile bird feeders. Corn, apples, and other goodies will keep them occupied. You can serve the food directly on the ground or in a sturdily built tray feeder. Deer will also regularly visit a salt block.

Setting up a separate feeding station for deer is a good idea only if you have a large property— and can offer their food far away from your garden.

Should deer run out of eats at their feeding station, they will devour millet, birdseed mix, and just about any other grain-based foods at your other feeders.

Keep in mind that deer are browsers. They nip off the twigs and tips of many garden plants and trees. If you invite deer to your yard, they may quickly become a nuisance and injure your treasured plantings. Unless you have a very large property where deer naturally dwell and can supply their food far away from favorite garden areas, it's probably best not to open the door to the potential problems they can cause.

To discourage deer permanently, you'll have to resort to the same methods that gardeners use. The only fail-safe solution is a high fence around your yard. High plastic netting is effective and much less expensive than wire or wood, and its dark color blends in with the background so that you hardly notice it. Tie strips of white cloth to the fence at first so that deer don't blunder into it accidentally. A dog is also a great deterrent to deer.

An interesting low-tech solution to deer at the feeder is to fill your

DEER FEEDER FOODS
at a glance

IF you're kind enough to set up a separate feeding station for deer in your yard, you can keep them happy by serving:

- Acorns
- American persimmons
- Apples
- Beechnuts
- Bread and other baked goodies
- Cereal
- Corn
- Crackers
- Salt

feeders with seed treated with capsaicin, the fiery stuff of hot peppers. Birds don't mind the substance in the least, but mammals are sensitive to the burning effects and will eat pepper-coated seed only as a last resort.

Birdbaths

A BOOK on feeding and feeders just wouldn't be complete without a mention of birdbaths. Water is as big a draw for birds as food, especially in summer when dry weather makes natural water hard to find. Many birds have become accustomed to seeking birdbaths to get a drink of water and have a refreshing splash.

Common backyard birds like chickadees, house finches, goldfinches, grackles, robins, and house sparrows will readily use an old-fashioned concrete birdbath—the simple basin balanced atop a sturdy pedestal. Other birds, generally the shyer types that live in woodlands or large, open natural areas, are difficult to tempt to the unfamiliar height and structure of a birdbath. You can increase your bath's appeal by lowering it. Place the basin at ground level to entice the birds that usually drink from puddles and streams.

You can try another tactic and make the landscape around the bath more inviting to shy birds than the typical wide-open expanse of lawn that usually surrounds the birdbath. Groups of shrubs or bushes or other corridors of safety will encourage birds to approach without feeling unsafe from exposure.

Safe Haven

WHEN planting around a birdbath, you need to create a careful balance between shelter and safety. While you want to have a place for wet birds to perch, you also want to make sure those birds have a clear view of approaching danger.

Cats are a real menace around a birdbath. If a stalking kitty is plaguing your birds and you can't exclude the animal from your yard, it's best to keep an open area of at least 10 feet around the bath. That should give birds enough time to become airborne once they spot the stalker. Beyond the bare zone, plant shrubs for birds to dive into for safety.

BATHING SPACE

Concrete birdbaths are a real value for the money. Expect to pay about $20 for a fine, classic model that will last for many years. Because the basin may break, you can also buy the top and bottom sections separately. (You could also buy just the basins, and then set them directly on the ground or on a low stack of bricks.)

Large, shallow clay saucers, sold for catching drips beneath potted plants, also are ideal for birdbaths. Comparison-shop before you buy—a standard birdbath basin may cost less than a clay saucer, and it will hold up to the ravages of weather much longer.

Plastic plant saucers are another option, although they may be too slippery for the birds' comfort. (You can try roughing them up with very coarse sandpaper to give birds something to grip.) At a cost of just a couple of dollars each, they're a great way to provide water, and they can withstand freezing and thawing. Keep a few on hand to rotate in the winter—when one freezes up, bring it in to thaw and replace it with a freshly filled saucer.

YEAR-ROUND USE

Birdbaths are popular all year because resident birds soon learn to depend on an always-available supply of fresh water. The very presence of birds at the bath may lure stopover migrants, even without the addition of a pump or mister to create water music.

Although the dry season is when birds utilize birdbaths the most, winter in cold areas is also a popular time for birdbaths. As freezing temperatures turn natural water sources to solid ice, birds will become loyal visitors at a birdbath with open water. If you live in a cold-winter area, it's well worth investing a few dollars in additional aids to keep your birdbath ice-free.

A submersible electric heater, which sells for about $20, is the top de-icer choice of most backyard

> **Birds won't be your only customers at a birdbath. Chipmunks, squirrels, toads, and butterflies will also benefit from the fresh water.**

birders. In severe cold, don't expect the heater to keep the entire container unfrozen. It may allow only the part of the water very near the heater to stay in a liquid state in frigid weather. Birds will quickly find the open water.

Solar-heated birdbaths are also available. They depend on the warmth of the sun to keep the dark plastic dish ice-free. If your winter weather is mostly overcast as well as icy cold, a solar-heated bath won't be very effective.

TIDYING UP

Like any pool of stagnant water, a birdbath can harbor a fine crop of algae if you let it go without cleaning for several days. Even worse than the slimy stuff is the fact that a birdbath is the perfect breeding place for mosquito larvae. That said, you really do need to clean a birdbath frequently.

Any abrasive will get rid of algae. You can use a plastic scouring pad, a scrap of sandpaper, a handful of sand, or a scrub brush. To save steps on cleaning chores, you can keep your scrubbies inside the hollow pedestal of the birdbath. Loop a wire around the top of the pedestal and through the handle of the brush or corner of the scouring pad. When you're ready to clean, tilt the basin to empty it, lift it from the pedestal, and fish out your scrubbing tool. Before refilling the basin with fresh water, drop the tool back into the pedestal.

4
CREATING A GREEN SCENE

Best Flowers, Fruit, Trees, and Shrubs for the Birds

PUTTING OUT THE WELCOME MAT for birds means more than offering their favorite foods at the feeder. Birds love a diversity of plants in the backyard as well. Flowers, trees, shrubs, ornamental grasses, and groundcovers entice birds with their promise of food, shelter, protection, and nesting materials. As you garden with birds in mind, you'll see that the two go naturally hand in hand. You'll end up with a lush landscape filled with birds to watch for your enjoyment, and the birds will keep coming back for all that your gardens have to offer.

Flowers for Birds

YOU probably choose the flowers you grow based on color or fragrance. But birds have an entirely different agenda when it comes to their floral favorites. If you want to use your flower garden to tempt birds into visiting your yard, look for flowering plants that provide edible seeds, useful nesting materials, or shelter for safety and nesting. Except for nectar-sipping orioles and hummingbirds, birds are uninterested in the blossoms themselves unless they attract small insects, another mainstay on the bird menu.

More is better when it comes to bird gardens. A single potted plant won't attract much, if any, avian attention. But a wide bed with a variety of plants is bound to be a popular spot, thanks to the insects that live among the leaves, branches, and flowers. Those aphids you despise are a delicious appetizer to chickadees; your plump tomato hornworms are as desirable as prime rib to a brown thrasher. Even the Japanese beetles devouring your roses are appealing to foraging birds.

FLOWERS FOR FOOD

Keep in mind that a yard filled with flowers attracts zillions of insects, which are manna to birds. Even if you're growing flowers in your garden that don't yield seeds or fruits for bird dining, they'll still add something for hungry birds to munch on. Daisies (*Chrysanthemum* spp.), oregano (*Origanum vulgare*), yarrows (*Achillea* spp.), and other flowering plants that produce clusters of many tiny nectar-rich flowers are best for attracting the small insects that bring in the birds.

If you hope to grow seeds for your feathered friends along with your flowers, start with annuals. Annuals are prolific seed producers. Perennial flowers tend to be stingier with their seeds, but some, such as purple coneflower (*Echinacea purpurea*), are worthwhile from a bird's point of view.

Flowering weeds are also great for the bird garden: Common chicory, goldenrod, and dandelion-like hawkweed are just a few of the weeds that help feed the birds. (For more on weeds that birds like, see page 174.)

FLOWERS FOR NESTS

Plant fibers and twigs are two top components of many bird nests. If you let your garden plants stand over winter, their stems will be weathered just right for birds to strip long lengths of fiber from them at spring nesting time.

Any perennial or annual flower with stiff, slim, twiggy branches is a prime candidate for nesting material. If you can bring yourself to delay spring cleanup, you can watch birds collecting sticks or stringy leaves from many garden flowers, including bearded iris (*Iris* bearded hybrids), Siberian iris (*I. siberica*), and mallows (*Hibiscus* and *Malva* spp.). If you prefer a tidy garden, collect the stalks of fibrous plants and pile them beside your compost pile for orioles to harvest at nesting time.

FLOWERS FOR SHELTER

A densely planted flower garden that features tall, branching plants as well as clumps of plants closer to the ground provides useful shelter to birds in your backyard. Lush

Designing for the Birds

WHEN it comes to designing a garden for birds, you'll want to provide food and protective cover first because these two work hand in hand to tempt birds into lingering in your yard. Begin by considering where birds spend their time in the wild and where they hunt for food naturally. Then apply those insights to your flower garden plan, keeping in mind what birds you want to attract.

■ Robins and a few other birds, like grackles and starlings, appreciate a sparsely planted garden with neatly weeded space between the plants because that gives them easy access to open soil for pulling worms and finding bugs.

■ Grosbeaks, orioles, tanagers, vireos, warblers, and other birds that spend most of their time in the trees are lured to lower levels by abundant fruit or insects—their favorite foods. They prefer to stick close to cover, so make sure your flowerbeds form a corridor that leads to and from the safety of trees.

■ Buntings and native sparrows are low on the food chain, so they spend most of their time in thick vegetation. In the wild, they stay in the brushy edges of fields and roadsides. In your flower garden, they'll appreciate plenty of taller, branching plants that mimic the shrubs in their wild habitat.

■ Cardinals, catbirds, mockingbirds, and wrens aren't as shy as other songbirds because they're accustomed to living around people. But densely planted flowers of varying heights will keep them safe while they search for food in your garden.

Also keep in mind plants that the birds will love. You can grow a birdseed garden with these annuals (you can sow them directly in your garden):

■ Love-lies-bleeding (*Amaranthus caudatus*)

■ Bachelor's button (*Centaruea cyanus*)

■ 'Rosa' cosmos (*Cosmos bipinnatus* 'Rosa')

■ 'Lemon Queen' sunflowers (*Helianthus* spp.)

■ Garden balsam (*Impatiens balsamina*)

flower gardens give birds a place to wait out rain and wind. If the flowers are near your feeders, birds can use the flowerbed as an escape route in case of predators. Be aware that cats may also use flowers near feeders as cover for sneaking up on birds. If cats are a problem in your yard, keep the flowers at least 6 feet from the feeders.

Birds that spend most of their lives on or near the ground may even become residents of your flower garden. Buntings, native sparrows, and common yellow-throats are the birds most likely to turn up because they aren't as shy as others when it comes to human interference. In relatively undisturbed corners, you may also find thrushes and towhees making themselves at home.

Ground-nesting birds like to snuggle their woven cups against a dense clump of grass or among thick plant stems, where they're hidden from view. Flowers that grow into shrub-size plants or those that form thick colonies are ideal nesting sites for indigo buntings and the common yellow-throat. Song sparrows often nest among daylilies (*Hemerocallis* spp.) and in groundcovers, while white-crowned sparrows favor lupines (*Lupinus* spp.).

You can provide shelter as well as food for birds by planting flowers such as purple coneflower, black-eyed Susan, Russian sage, and lupine.

Annuals

ANNUALS are great bird attractors—in addition to being fast and easy to grow. If you don't want to bother planting annual seeds, just visit your local garden center, where you're sure to find your favorites in pots or flats, ready to plant.

The colors and scents of annual flowers are a season-long delight. When you grow annuals, you can cut armloads of blossoms for indoor bouquets. And even if you forget to water and weed, your annuals will often bloom nonstop till frost.

Plant annuals densely because birds feel more at home in thick growth. You can plant transplants or sow seeds directly in the garden. Keep the seedbed moist until the seedlings are established, and mulch with compost before the annuals start to flower.

Seeds for Winter Feeding

ANNUALS become even more attractive to birds as summer ends. When cosmos and zinnias go to seed, they become a feeding station for many beautiful birds. Goldfinches will hang from the tips of cosmos, stretching to nibble the slim black seeds.

An old-fashioned annual called love-lies-bleeding (*Amaranthus caudatus*) has unusual dangling "ropes" of deep pink flowers that look like fat lengths of fuzzy yarn. After the flowers mature, they yield thousands of tiny oil-rich seeds that native sparrows and finches adore. Another old-time favorite, the humble bachelor's-button (*Centaurea cyanus*) attracts finches, buntings, and native sparrows when its flowers to go seed. Because bachelor's-button flowers mature at different times, you're apt to see goldfinches and other birds foraging for seeds even while the plant is still blooming.

When the garden season ends, don't be too quick to cut back your annuals. Leave them standing in the garden during the winter. Juncos and native sparrows will scratch beneath them, gleaning leftover seed that has dropped to the ground.

COSMOS

In the wild, as in the garden, this aster family member appeals to all kinds of seed-eating birds, from cardinals to doves to sparrows. Plant it in masses in full sun near your feeding station or outside your favorite window, where you can watch the crowds of birds that arrive to dine on its seeds. Look carefully to spot goldfinches, which blend in surprisingly well among the flowers and foliage; a bending stem is sometimes the only telltale clue to their presence.

Like other bird favorites, cosmos can stand all winter long in the garden. Even though this annual is killed off by frost, its ferny stems still provide shelter, and birds will work on its seedheads all through the winter months.

The seeds of both yellow, orange, or red cosmos (*C. sulphureus*) and pink, red, or white cosmos (*C. bipinnatus*) are yummy to birds. These heat-loving annual plants can take a long time to flower, a drawback in short-season areas, where they may just hit their peak when killing frost arrives. To encourage faster bloom, grow them in lean soil with no fertilizer.

Collect cosmos stems after the flowers go to seed and use them in outdoor wreaths for the birds. Some seed eaters will perch on the wreath to dine, while ground-feeding birds such as doves, sparrows, and towhees will congregate beneath the wreath, where they'll quickly clean up any dropped seeds. Birds are bound to miss some that fall to the ground, and those seeds will sprout the following spring to produce a new year's round of flowers and seeds.

Sow a patch of cosmos in your yard and you'll be delighted by the number of seed-eating birds that stop by for a bite.

FLAX

Extremely delicate, with small needle-like leaves on a fine stem topped by a cluster of silky, sky blue flowers, flax is a beautiful garden flower as well as a favorite of finches. It also produces the fiber used to make linen fabric.

Flaxseed is ultrahigh in oil. Use the back of your thumbnail to press one of the flat, shiny brown seeds against a piece of paper and you'll see a greasy smear. That's great news for buntings, goldfinches, purple finches, and other small, high-energy birds who seek out the high-calorie seeds to keep their active bodies stoked with fuel.

Annual flax (*Linum usitatissimum*) is simple to grow in a sunny spot. Scatter the seeds thickly over prepared soil, press into the soil, and wait for a field of blue flowers to appear. Let it stand in bloom, and as the flowers fade, it will attract birds for months.

Most birdseed dealers sell flax seed only as part of a high-priced mix. Check with your closest feed mill or farm-supply store to see if you can buy the seed at bulk prices, which will save you a bundle when you make your own custom birdseed blends.

IMPATIENS

Impatiens are the perfect plants for brightening shady places with bloom from spring through frost

Perennial Flax

PERENNIAL flax species are also attractive to birds, even though their seeds aren't as abundant as those of most annual species. The plant most commonly known as perennial flax, *Linum perenne*, is a popular garden flower because of its graceful appearance and pretty sky blue flowers. Its clumps of wiry stems are clothed in delicate needle-like foliage. Like annual flax, its blossoms open in the morning and close by afternoon, except on cloudy days. The lookalike prairie flax (*L. perenne* subsp. *lewisii*) of western North America has a slightly more robust look, as does the species *L. narbonense*, which is gaining popularity in perennial gardens.

with never a letup—and they bring hummingbirds calling wherever you plant them. Impatiens are a well-loved favorite for flowerbeds, but bird-loving gardeners should also plant pots or hanging baskets of impatiens for a close-up look at the hummingbirds that feed at the nectar-rich flowers. As a bonus, when impatiens go to seed, you can watch rose-breasted grosbeaks, sparrows, finches, and buntings feed on the seeds.

Impatiens (*Impatiens wallerana*) are a tender perennial usually treated as an easy-care annual. They come in enough colors to suit any color scheme. Plant a six-pack of impatiens, and the plants will quickly fill out into mounds of lance-shaped green or bronze leaves from 6 to 12 inches tall, covered with hundreds of 1- to 2-inch-wide cheery flowers.

New Guinea impatiens (*I. hawkeri*) are taller and flashier than regular impatiens. They have dazzling, boldly striped leaves of green, bronze, pink, red, and yellow. New Guinea impatiens reach 2 feet tall, and the pink, red, orange, purple, or white flowers are 3 inches across.

GROWING IMPATIENS at a glance

Hands down, impatiens are the best flower for shade. They also grow in sun but may wilt in dry soil and midday heat.

■ Plant impatiens in soil that's well amended with organic matter, and keep the soil moist (but not soggy).

■ Use starter plants because seeds are slow to germinate (they can take as long as 3 weeks) and to grow.

■ Space compact types 6 to 10 inches apart and larger varieties 15 to 20 inches apart.

■ To multiply your impatiens, simply snip cuttings from mature plants and insert them into moist soil, where they'll quickly root.

SAFFLOWER

Vivid orange safflower (*Cartha-mus tinctorius*) blossoms are definite attention getters in a garden of birdseed plants. This annual is easy to grow from seed sown directly in sunny soil, and birds will come flocking once its flower heads mature into small, plump white seeds. At the feeder, cardinals are the main customer for safflower seeds. It may take the red birds a while to discover the seeds, but once they do, they'll be regulars at the feeder. Packaged cardinal seed mix is often nothing more than black sunflower seeds mixed with white safflower—a fine combination tailor-made for cardinal tastes but usually much less expensive to blend yourself from sunflower and saffron seed bought in bulk.

> **Try safflower seed in your feeder if you prefer not to host jays—they're generally not very interested in eating it. Squirrels will usually pass up this seed as well.**

If your cardinals aren't used to eating safflower, start with just a scant handful of the seeds sprinkled atop a tray of black oil sunflower seeds. Once you can see that the birds have started eating the safflower seeds, you can increase the servings. Safflower seed is a good choice if you prefer not to host jays at your feeder because they're generally not interested in it. With any luck, they'll depart for better vittles at another bird café when you switch to feeding mainly safflower. Squirrels don't care for safflower, either, and will bypass a feeder filled with it to seek their food elsewhere.

SUNFLOWERS

Sunflowers are the number-one plant for a bird-friendly backyard. They're easy to grow, and birds will begin feasting on the seeds while the sunflowers are still blooming—as soon as the meaty kernels plump up. Cardinals, jays, finches, buntings, sparrows, chickadees, woodpeckers, grosbeaks, nuthatches, and titmice will harvest the seeds for months. At season's end, you can harvest sunflower heads and hang them from a porch post for birds to eat, or use them to make festive bird treats.

Although you can still find the classic tall, single-headed sunflower on seed racks and in garden catalogs, you'll also see a fantastic range of new sunflowers, all selected from the parent species, *Helianthus annus,* the common sunflower.

You can grow sunflowers in dramatic autumnal shades of rust and copper; in pint-sized versions with full-size blooms on knee-high plants; with fluffy, double flowers that look more like a cactus-flowered zinnia than a sunflower; and in varieties that are pollen-free

so that cut flowers don't dust your end table with a golden shower. You can even grow ancient varieties that were bred by native Americans, with seeds of burnished chestnut, deep charcoal-blue, or creamy white.

As far as birds are concerned, tasty seeds are the main reason for growing sunflowers. So choose the varieties that appeal to your personal preference, as long as they bear a bountiful crop. How can you tell? The birds will let you know. If cardinals, chickadees, goldfinches, titmice, or other sunflower eaters aren't perched on the seedheads after the petals wither, you've planted a dud.

Perennial Sunflowers

NORTH America, the home of sunflowers, boasts dozens of species of native perennial sunflowers. The flower heads are much smaller than those of the annual sunflower, but they're still crammed with small, bird-attracting seeds. All have sunny yellow daisy flowers on plants of varying height, form, and foliage. Maximilian sunflower (*H. maximilianii*), for instance, is a regal plant, stretching 8 feet or taller, with flowers borne thickly along the top 2 feet of each stem. Soft sunflower (*H. mollis*), on the other hand, tends to flop or recline against neighboring plants. Its velvet-soft gray foliage and clusters of furred buds are as pretty as its buttery yellow flowers, which usually appear about 2 feet from ground level.

plants

Cosmos Impatiens Sunflowers Zinnias Bee balm Columbine Fuchsias Vines Trees Shrubs

Plants that sprout from dropped birdseed also produce excellent seeds for birds, but the plant won't look like their parents. Instead, they'll have stout, single stems, and the flower heads may be much less flashy-looking. These volunteer plants are the same type of sunflower that decorates roadsides from Missouri to the Rockies each summer in a wide swath of shining yellow. If you're experimenting with new varieties, do your birds a favor and find a spot where you can plant some plain old birdseed sunflowers for insurance, just in case your prettified plants don't produce good seeds.

By planting annual sunflowers, you'll create an instant birdseed garden.

ZINNIAS

Zinnias (*Zinnia* spp.) are one of the easiest annual flowers to grow—and that's good news for bird lovers. Zinnias have bright, daisylike flowers that attract a bounty of butterflies when they're in full bloom, but that's only the beginning. Red- and orange-flowered zinnias also lure hummingbirds to their nectar. And when the flower heads begin to go to seed, goldfinches are first on the scene. If you leave your zinnia patch standing through fall and into winter, you'll spot buntings, doves, native sparrows, and towhees, busily scratching for seeds around the plants.

Zinnias take only 10 to 12 weeks to burst into bloom, counting from the time you plant the seeds. They flourish in full sun,

Grow a Garden Full of Birdseed

WATCHING birds eating natural foods in a garden is even more fun than watching birds at a feeder. And a garden filled with plants that produce delectable seeds will last longer than any tray of offerings you put out. Seeds of annual flowers like zinnias mature for months as new flowers keep opening, so there's a bounty of food. And in winter, when pickings are slimmer, birds will still visit the garden to glean overlooked seeds from the ground and from almost-empty seedheads.

Most birdseed plants are annuals, so planting a birdseed garden offers quick gratification. If you start a birdseed garden in spring, by summer the birds will be reaping the rewards. Naturally, annuals for birds are plants that produce lots of seeds, so after the first year the garden will resprout on its own accord.

To grow a garden full of birdseed, plant:

- 'Golden Goddess' tickseed sunflower (*Bidens aristosa* 'Golden Goddess')
- Bachelor's-button (*Centaurea cyanus*)
- 'Sensation Mix' cosmos (*Cosmos bipinnatus* 'Sensation Mix')
- Yellow cosmos (*C. sulphureus*)
- Purple coneflower (*Echinacea purpurea*)
- 'Autumn Beauty' common sunflower (*Helianthus annuus* 'Autumn Beauty')
- Saw-toothed sunflower (*H. grosseserratus*)
- Switch grass (*Panicum virgatum*)
- Creeping zinnia (*Sanvitalia procumbens*)
- Foxtail millet (*Setaria italica*)
- 'Persian Carpet' zinnia (*Zinnia haageana* 'Persian Carpet')

Hummingbird Magnets

SALVIA blossoms are tailor-made for hummingbird beaks. The vividly colored, small, tubular blossoms of both annual and perennial salvias add long-lasting color to your garden and provide a feast for nectar-seeking hummingbirds.

Salvias run the gamut in size, form, and flower color. They have square stems, showing that they belong to the mint family. But unlike mints, salvias don't spread rampantly. Some cultivars, such as 'East Friesland', are neat plants that stay in a compact mound about 1 foot tall. At the other end of the scale are salvias like clary sage (*Salvia sclarea*) that stretch out into 3-foot shrubs. Be sure to give sprawling salvias like these plenty of room and to support them, and string stakes if the plants flop.

Many salvias are native to the western deserts, so they prefer well-drained, light or loose soil and an open, airy location. However, some salvias grow as well in average garden soil as they do in less-fertile soil. All salvias do best in full sun. In cold areas, grow the more tender salvias as annuals, or bring potted plants or rooted cuttings indoors before the first frost to over-winter on your sunniest windowsills.

If you want to advertise a garden buffet to hummingbirds, start with three fire-engine red salvias: scarlet sage (*S. splendens*), pineapple sage (*S. elegans*), and Texas sage (*S. coccinea*). These sages will reach from 1 to 3 feet tall when grown as annuals. Scarlet sage and pineapple sage are tender perennials that can reach up to 8 feet high in Zones 9 and 10. Autumn salvia (*S. greggii*) is a perennial salvia that grows from 1 to 3 feet tall and is hardy enough to overwinter in Zones 7 to 10. Pineapple sage and autumn salvia bloom very late in the season, so protect them from early frosts by covering the plants with a sheet on cold nights.

Red doesn't have to be the only salvia color on your hummingbird buffet. If you like blue flowers, salvias are definitely the way to go—some of the hardiest perennial salvias have blue flowers. These include blue sage (*S. azurea*), pitcher's sage (*S. azurea* var. *grandiflora*), and meadow sage (*S. pratensis*).

in rich or lean soil, and in clay or sandy places. Traditional cactus-flowered or double-flowered zinnias (*Z. elegans*) are excellent for songbirds, hummingbirds, and butterflies; for smaller seed-eating species, the lower-growing zinnia cultivars 'Bonita Red' and 'Bonita Yellow' or old-fashioned Persian carpet (*Z. haageana*) are tops.

Zinnias are prone to powdery mildew, which causes a whitish dusting on their foliage. The effect is cosmetic: It's not fatal to the plants, and flowers are usually unaffected. Because mildew is most noticeable when the plant is a tall one, you might add midheight and dwarf zinnia cultivars in front of your giants to hide their foliage, just in case it becomes disfigured. Or you can stick to planting mildew-resistant cultivars.

If you plant a large sweep of zinnias, you can easily snip off seedheads and offer them in feeders later in the season, or work them into a wreath for birds. Try cutting the ripe seedheads with long stems attached, tie them together with twine, and attach them to a lamppost, fence post, or door—they'll attract cardinals, tit-

mice, and other birds. Save some of the seeds for planting next year. If you save seed of named cultivars, you may find the next generation doesn't look very much like its parents. If your garden color scheme is important, sow the saved seeds in an out-of-the-way spot, where a sudden unexpected jolt of fuchsia or scarlet won't disrupt your soft pastels.

Zinnias are great flowers for first-time gardeners: They sprout in just a few days, the seedlings are big and hearty, and they grow fast and bloom quickly.

(And if you want to give a child a love of gardening, pass along a packet or two of zinnia seeds. They're as close to foolproof as gardening gets.)

Colorful and foolproof, zinnias will attract butterflies and hummingbirds all summer long. Other birds will come to feast in fall, when the flower heads begin to go to seed.

Creating a Green Scene

Q I've noticed that wheat seed is a common ingredient in birdseed mixes. If I grow my own wheat, will my backyard birds nibble on it?

A Although birds usually scorn wheat in the feeder—unless it's the last resort—blackbirds, doves, grouse, pheasants, quail, and house sparrows will seek it out on the stem or forage for dropped kernels when the grain matures.

Wheat is a pretty addition to a birdseed garden. The long bristles on the seed kernels catch the light and lend a delicate, silky look to plantings. All wheat is simple to grow. Scratch up a planting bed, scatter the seed kernels, cover them lightly, keep the bed watered, and in a few days you'll have a thick crop sprouting and growing fast.

Q I have a relatively small garden and am thinking about adding a few trellises around my bird-feeding area—not only to supply more growing room for plants but also to offer shade and shelter to the feeder birds. Do you have any suggestions as to some plants that would work best for these purposes?

A Choose plants to cover arbors and trellises using the same criteria as you would for other plantings in your bird-friendly yard. Select those that do double duty, offering a food source as well as shelter.

Native vines are an excellent choice for bird arbors because they have evolved along with the birds that use them. Their fruits ripen when birds need them most, and the tasty treats they provide stay edible into winter. For example, American bittersweet (*Celastrus scandens*) is a tough, twining vine hardy to Zone 2 that has bright orange-and-red fruits.

Virginia creeper (*Parthenocissus quinquefolia*) is hardy to Zone 3 and has clusters of deep blue berries on bright red stems.

Perennials

PERENNIALS are the backbone of the garden, returning year after year to provide colorful flowers, attractive foliage, and dinner for the birds. Some perennials like coneflowers offer tasty seeds, whereas coral bells and others provide nectar for hummingbirds. But the biggest benefit of perennials to birds isn't their seeds—it's the plants themselves. Perennials provide excellent cover so birds can move safely through the garden, and their foliage holds insects, caterpillars, slugs, snails, and other ready-to-eat goodies.

BEE BALM

Bee balm (*Monarda didyma*) belongs to the mint family, and you know what that means: This plant is pushy. It's a spreading perennial that can quickly shoulder aside its neighbors. Plant a small division or pot of bee balm in spring, and by season's end it will have spread to 2 feet or more. If you have loose, fertile soil, you may have a 6-foot circle of bee balm by the end of its second year of growth. (It's also easy to keep bee balm in place—its knotted, lateral roots pull up like a rug.)

Bee balm is a native of eastern North America and grows wild along woodland streams. In gardens it thrives in Zones 4 to 8, growing well in sun or partial shade and in almost any soil. The unusual mop-head flowers often have a tiered arrangement, each tier made up of a circle of individual tubular flowers.

More Bee Balms

WILD bergamot (*Monarda fistulosa*) is a native bee balm of dry, open fields. It has pale purple-pink flowers, grows well in dry soils in Zones 3 to 9, and is lovely in a meadow garden. Spotted bee balm (*M. punctata*) is another good hummingbird plant that thrives in Zones 3 to 9. It has light yellow flowers with purple spots.

If you don't have any hummers frequenting your garden yet, plant a red bee balm such as 'Cambridge Scarlet', 'Adam', or 'Gardenview Scarlet'. Their brilliant color will draw hummingbirds like magic. Once hummingbirds find your garden, they'll also linger at bee balms of other colors.

COLUMBINES

Hummingbirds relish columbines. The jewel-toned birds hover above columbine flowers like helicopters as they slip their slender beaks into the long "spurs" of each blossom to reach its sweet nectar. If you haven't attracted hummers to your yard yet, put out the welcome sign by planting red-and-yellow-flowered wild columbine (*Aquilegia canadensis*) and its cousin, the pretty crimson columbine (*A. formosa*).

Plant columbine seeds in full sun to light or part shade in average to fertile, well-drained soil. For best flowering, dig in a generous helping of compost or other organic matter before you plant.

Columbines are long-blooming but not long-lived. The parent plants peter out after a few years, but volunteer seedlings usually spring up to take their place.

Columbines look best planted in drifts. The flowers open from spring through early summer, and the ground-hugging fernlike foliage forms a beautiful dense blue-green carpet, flourishing even in dry shade beneath trees or rocky areas.

You can choose from species and cultivars ranging in size from 6-inch mounds to plants that grow 3 feet tall and wide. Some good choices include golden columbine

Entice hummingbirds to your garden with the blossoms of Rocky Mountain columbine.

Offering Coreopsis

THE prairie flowers of the genus *Coreopsis* include annual and perennial species, all of them loaded with tasty bird-attracting seeds. Other coreopsis hail from desert homes in North and Central America, so no matter where you live, you'll discover rewarding native coreopsis that are appropriate for your garden conditions. Members of the giant aster family, these bright daisies are usually yellow, with the exceptions of calliopsis (*C. tinctoria*), which also blooms in burgundy and bicolors, and pink tickseed (*C. rosea*), a pink-flowered species.

Native sparrows appear most often when coreopsis seeds are on the menu, although other birds also enjoy them. Look for white-crowned and white-throated sparrows among the plants in fall and winter. Towhees may scratch underneath to turn up overlooked bits of seeds, and doves and quail will also forage beneath the plants.

Calliopsis (*C. tinctoria*), a self-sowing annual once used as a dye plant, produces so many seeds—thanks to its dozens of blooms—that you can easily harvest the seed for winter feeding. Snip sprays of the seedheads and weave their thin, wiry stems into wreaths and swags for a decorative bird treat.

All coreopsis are easy to grow in a sunny site in average, well-drained soil. Hardiness varies by species. Two of the easiest and most widely adaptable perennial species are *C. lanceolata* and *C. grandiflora,* dependable performers with bouquets of sunny golden flowers. Start the seeds indoors in late winter for some bloom the same year. Expect to see butterflies at the flowers of any coreopsis you grow.

(*A. chrysantha*), which has big, long-spurred, sulfur yellow flowers, and Rocky Mountain columbine (*A. caerulea*), with its airy blue flowers.

CONEFLOWERS

No self-respecting bird garden should be without coneflowers. These long-blooming perennials have daisylike flowers with centers that stick up like the crowns of Mexican sombreros. And those high-hat centers are packed with nutritious seeds for backyard birds like finches, sparrows, and buntings.

These easy-to-grow perennials flourish in poor soil or rich loam. They're hardy over a wide range, most types at least from Zones 4 to 9. Coneflowers are usually untroubled by pests and diseases, take the worst droughts in stride, and rarely need dividing. Best of all, they bloom their heads off for most of the summer, year after year.

Coneflowers are easy to grow from seeds. Sow the seeds in a sunny spot in well-drained, average garden soil, and keep the soil evenly moist until the young plants have several sets of leaves. After

that they need watering only when the soil dries out. These knee-high to waist-high flowers are also beautiful combined with other meadow flowers or with ornamental grasses like feather reed grass (*Calamagrostis acutiflora*). And any coneflower seeds the birds don't eat will self-sow to spread the beauty.

The common black-eyed Susan (*Rudbeckia hirta*) reaches 2 to 3 feet tall, and its branching steams and dense leaves offer small birds safe shelter where they can forage for insects or seeds. Plant several near your feeding station to encourage buntings, finches, sparrows, and other small birds to linger within view. Black-eyed Susans will attract a flurry of butterflies to your yard, too, and they're pretty and long-lasting in bouquets. Even after black-eyed Susans lose their golden petals, their dark central cones will stand tall atop the stiff stems, holding up their cache of seeds for hungry birds. If you must clean up the faded flowers, gather them into bunches to hang from a feeder or weave them into a wreath of bird-seed treats. Easy to grow and drought-tolerant, these plants thrive in Zones 3 through 10.

Other worthy coneflowers include purple coneflower (*Echinacea purpurea*), which is one of the longest-blooming perennials, shining coneflower (*Rudbeckia nitida*), brown-eyed Susan (*R. triloba*), and cut-leaved coneflower (*R. laciniata*).

You can also plant prairie coneflowers (*Ratibida* spp.), which have wilder-looking flowers than black-eyed Susans. Their petals droop and are often widely spaced around the raised center like a gap-toothed smile.

CORAL BELLS

Coral bells are delicate, but they pack a big punch with hummingbirds. Coral bells (*Heuchera san-*guinea and *H.* × *brizoides*) sport tiny red, pink, white, or salmon blossoms that dangle above the foliage like fringed bells in late spring. If you clip off old flowerstalks when the blossoms fade, the plants will continue pushing up new flowering stems for months. But even when they're not in bloom, the 1- to 2½-foot-tall mounds of foliage add an air of tidiness to the garden. Some types have fancy leaves ranging from bright green to nearly black, with splotches of silver and pink, or red veining.

Plant coral bells at the fronts of your borders and along the edges of paths in rich, loose, well-drained, moist soil. If you're cursed with clay soil, lighten it up with plenty of leaf mold and compost to

Attracting Live Bird Food

ALL coneflowers attract butterflies and other insects, so when they're in flower, they bring in live bird food, too. Small butterflies on their way to and from the plants are likely to be quickly snatched up by flycatchers or English sparrows, and smaller insects become a quick dinner for any wrens in the neighborhood. Because coneflowers attract so many insects, they also attract predatory spiders that often stretch their webs across the branches of the plants. The spiderwebs, in turn, may attract hummingbirds that will flit about, collecting the sticky webs for building their nests.

make your coral bells happy. These hardy perennials (Zones 3 to 8) do best in full sun in the North, but in the South, they'll live longer in sites with partial or afternoon shade.

FUCHSIAS

Fuchsias will dress up your garden or your front porch all summer with their 3-inch-long, dangling "ladies' earrings" flowers in vibrant shades of purple, violet, red, pink, white, or flashy two-tones. The tubular flowers of fuchsias (*Fuchsia* × *hybrida*) are sure to entice hummingbirds, who often claim territorial rights to an individual plant and fend off competing hummers with dazzling displays of aerial warfare.

If you garden in a cold-winter area, you'll treat these tender perennials as summer plants, usually bought for the season and then discarded. Although some fuchsias can withstand Zone 6 winters, most cultivars are hardy only to Zone 8 or 9. Mild-winter gardeners can also grow shrubby hardy fuchsia (*F. magellanica*), which reaches the size of a forsythia bush in warm climates.

Hardy fuchsia can tolerate winters as cold as Zone 6 — it may die back to the ground in cold winters, but new growth quickly sprouts when warmer weather returns.

FLOWERING FUCHSIAS
at a glance

To keep your fuchsias flowering and the hummingbirds humming, follow these hints.

■ Set fuchsia plants in light shade and in average to fertile garden soil.

■ Keep the soil evenly moist.

■ Feed the plants every 10 days with a balanced liquid fertilizer, such as compost tea or fish emulsion.

■ In cold regions, pot up your plants and bring them indoors in fall.

Wildflowers

IT'S only natural that wild birds should love wildflowers. To them, wildflowers are living bird feeders that offer the ultimate in dining variety—seeds, nectar, and insects.

Because they tend to grow in dense, spreading colonies, wildflowers also help birds in another way: Dense wildflower foliage keeps birds safely out of sight as they move about on the forest floor or through a meadow.

WILDFLOWERS 101

Many of our favorite garden plants have wild roots, so it's easy to mix wildflowers into your garden with other perennials, annuals, and shrubs. Wiry-stemmed, simple-flowered oxeye daisies, for instance, are a close relative of bigger, more compact shasta daisies. They look great planted together, and both kinds are also fine companions for columbines and bearded irises in a perennial bed.

Most wildflowers adapt easily to life in a garden, as long as you are considerate of their light, soil, and drainage needs. Planting an all-wildflower patch is a rewarding project, too. If your yard is shady, wildflowers from the woods will light it up, especially in spring.

To choose the best wildflowers for birds, do a little birdwatching first. Visit local fields and woods, and check which native plants have seedheads that attract birds. Be sure to use them as the basis of your garden. Add in some tubular flowers like salvias to attract hummingbirds.

Each part of our country has native wildflowers that are a favorite with the birds of that region. By choosing plenty of natives, you're sure to create a bird-pleasing garden. Then add in some spreading wildflowers to provide good cover for the birds.

Wildflowers are perfect for providing cover for birds because they usually reproduce like rabbits. Perennial plants like yarrow and goldenrod and many other wildflowers have spreading roots that create ever-larger colonies of plants. Others, especially annual species such as calliopsis (*Coreopsis tinctoria*), produce prodigious amounts of seed to ensure the survival of their species.

STARTING FROM SCRATCH

If you decide to start a wildflower garden from scratch, you'll need to be sure you start it right. Keeping a meadow garden looking like those field-of-flower pictures you see on wildflower seed canisters can be a bit tricky. The showy annuals that add so much color to wildflower meadows are quickly choked out by perennial plants, like goldenrod and thistles.

To maintain a swath of colorful annual meadow flowers like bachelor's-buttons, poppies, and coreopsis, you'll need to keep the competition in check. That means starting out by preparing the soil thoroughly, and clearing out all bits of perennial weed roots that might sprout. Then each year you'll have to pull weeds that appear and cultivate the soil so that seeds that drop have open ground to sprout in.

For a meadow that maintains itself without so much coddling, switch to perennial flowers that spread quickly by roots. They can hold their own among invading weeds. Perennial sunflowers, coneflowers, agastache, bee balm, yarrow, and goldenrod are all pushy enough to keep a meadow garden looking good.

When you're gardening with wildflowers, never dig up plants from the wild. Stick with reputable nurseries or mail-order companies that grow their own wildflower plants. Ask whether they've propagated the plants themselves.

Price is one clue when you're shopping for wildflowers: If it seems too cheap to be true, the plants are most likely wild-collected. Most shade-loving wildflowers in particular multiply slowly, so expect them to be priced accordingly.

> **If you have a swampy spot in your lawn, plant moisture-loving wildflowers such as jewelweed, rushes, and great blue lobelia along the side of it.**

Top Wildflower Choices

Wildflowers of the aster family (Asteraceae) are top choices for birds. Sunflowers, coneflowers, coreopsis, and asters produce a bounty of nutritious seeds that sustain birds right through winter—plus they attract butterflies and other insects that birds eat. If you want to plant a wildflower garden just for the birds, consider incorporating the following plants:

New England aster (*Aster novae-angliae*). This popular plant bursts forth in royal purple glory in late summer. It reaches about 4 feet tall and thrives in Zones 4 to 8.

Calliopsis. Sparrows and finches love the seeds of this annual flower. Calliopsis (*Coreopsis tinctoria*) seeds abundantly, so even if birds come to feast on the seed, there's usually plenty left behind to self-sow for next year's garden. The delicate ferny foliage is splashed with a multitude of daisies in rich gold, burnt sienna, deep mahogany, or two-tone combinations of those colors. Plants can reach 3 feet tall in rich soil.

Coneflowers. Black-eyed Susans (*Rudbeckia* spp.) and purple coneflower (*Echinacea purpurea*) will keep your goldfinches happy when the seeds ripen in summer. Both types of coneflowers reach about 3 feet tall and grow well in Zones 3 to 8.

Sweet goldenrod. Goldenrods are notorious spreaders, and sweet goldenrod (*Solidago odora*) is no exception. But when you combine it with other vigorous perennials that can hold their own, it's gorgeous, making a splash of buttery yellow flowers in late summer. The plants have multiple stems that stand 3 to 4 feet tall and are hardy in Zones 3 to 9.

Great blue lobelia. One for the hummingbirds, great blue lobelia (*Lobelia siphilitica*) grows in a compact clump and bears dense spikes of blue flowers in late summer. It grows to about 2 feet tall and flourishes in Zones 4 to 8. It grows well in wet places but also thrives in average garden conditions.

Maximilian sunflower. Maximilian sunflowers (*Helianthus maximilianii*) can reach 8 feet or taller, depending on soil fertility. This sunflower spreads too quickly to work well in a perennial border, but it's perfect for a bird garden in Zones 5 to 9, where it can weave its gold among the other plants.

Creating a Green Scene

Q My backyard consists of a large lawn, with a few garden beds bordering the edges of it. I don't seem to have many birds frequenting my backyard, though. What am I missing?

A What you're missing is diversity—you have too much lawn. Robins and other birds that appreciate lawn space don't need an acre of mown grass to feel at home. A smaller patch suits them just fine. If you want more birds to visit, plan on reducing the size of your lawn. The birds will be happy, and you will be, too, because you'll spend less of your precious time on monotonous lawn care. Try planting a group of shrubs, a bed of groundcovers, or a corridor of flowers of varying heights. Or, replace an area of lawn with a meadow garden.

Q I recently moved into a new home and am wondering what to do with the stand of sumac at the back of my property. It's such a common wild plant that I don't feel it adds much to my landscape. But if it's bird-worthy, I might keep it. Any thoughts?

A Birds definitely love sumac—especially in winter. The plant's spires of fuzzy fruits provide long-term food in the leanest months of the year. Name a bird that dwells in your region, and it's a bet that it samples sumac fruits at some time from late fall to very early spring. When snowstorms move in with a vengeance, sumac is a natural for birds. The berries rarely go ignored in bad weather because their shape and position shrugs off most of the snow, so birds can reach them.

Roses

BIRDS don't care which rose smells best, but they do appreciate prickly canes, which can keep their nests safe from cats and other prowlers. Birds also enjoy feasting on the tasty orange or red fruits called rose hips, which can provide a winter's worth of nourishment.

Find a species rose like rugosa rose (*Rosa rugosa*), or one of the dozens of old-fashioned bushes, ramblers, and climbers, and chances are you'll find a song sparrow or cardinal nesting in its thorny branches and dozens of other birds stripping the clusters of rose hips in winter.

BLOOMS FOR THE BIRDS

Rugosa roses produce clusters of plump, colorful fruits, sometimes as big as cherries, that decorate the plants well into winter. Available with single or multipetaled flowers in shades of white, pink, purple, and red, these tough-as-nails roses thrive in spite of neglect. They grow as well in poor soil; in sandy, salty conditions; and during droughts as

they do when planted in a pampered garden setting. These ultra-hardy roses thrive in sun or part shade from Zone 7 to as far north as Zone 2.

The prairie rose (*R. setigera*) and the pasture rose (*R. carolina*), which is also called Carolina rose, are a pair of excellent native American roses with simple, single-petaled pink blossoms and fat, red rose hips. Both grow well in sun or part shade and adapt to most soils in Zones 4 through 8.

Other good roses to grow for bird snacks and shelter include the hardy meadow rose (*R. blanda*), which grows in Zones 2 to 7 and has rosy, single flowers and pear-shaped red hips. Sweetbrier (*R. eglanteria*) is hardy in Zones 4 to 8 and produces pale to deep pink flowers. The trailing or climbing memorial rose (*R. wichuraiana*), which grows in Zones 5 to 9, has pristine, white, multipetaled flowers and orange to dark red fruits. Don't overlook old shrub rose cultivars, such as the frilly, multipetaled pink 'Konigin von Danemark', which has dense branches and tasty rose hips.

Vines

VINES are a lush garden accent and a favorite hangout for backyard birds. The tangled stems and dense foliage of vines offer great roosting and nesting places. Fast-growing annual vines provide quick cover for a garden trellis and give birds a range of foods, from berries to insects. Woody perennial vines look beautiful covering an arbor and are sturdy enough to support nests. And the nectar-filled flowers of honeysuckle and other fragrant-flowered vines spice up your garden—some of them attract hummingbirds, too.

Here's a look at some of the best vines for the birds.

Annual Additions

HERE are some ideas for adding bird-attracting annual vines to your yard.

■ Easy-to-grow climbing beans are a terrific vine for birds. Plenty of insects like to feed on their foliage, and the birds will feast on those juicy morsels and feed them to their nestlings, too. The flowers of scarlet runner beans (*Phaseolus coccineus*) will bring hordes of hummingbirds to your yard.

■ Purple-flowered hyacinth bean (*Lablab purpurea*) is great for covering a wall of your house or a masonry retaining wall; its dense, high-climbing vines are so sturdy that birds may be tempted to nest there as well as seek shelter in them.

■ Climbing roses, while not truly vines, provide similar benefits for birds: a safe place to perch, plus insects on flowers and foliage, and tasty rosehips in the fall and winter. Climbing 'New Dawn' is one of the best because of its disease resistance and long, arching stems.

■ Birdhouse gourds, pumpkins, and squash cover fences and trellises with superfast greenery, and they offer a bonus at harvest time. You can make gourds into seed scoops, feeders, or birdhouses, while pumpkins and squash yield seeds for winter bird feeding.

ANNUAL VINES

Annual vines are real racehorses. Some, like moonflowers (*Ipomoea alba*), can blanket a wall in a single season. Others, such as feathery-leaved cypress vine (*I. quamoclit*), are delicate plants best grown on a trellis or over perennials and shrubs. Annual vines often grow the biggest in long-summer areas, where there's ample heat and humidity. Many types have seeds that germinate slowly. To speed germination, soak the seeds in warm water overnight before planting. A sunny spot of average, well-drained soil is all you need for success with annual vines. Avoid fertilizing, which encourages leafy growth and can delay flowering.

If your yard is short on shrubs and other permanent cover, install trellises of annual vines near your feeding station so that birds can make a quick getaway when danger threatens. Bathing birds will also appreciate a simple lattice trellis of annual vines near the birdbath, where they can find secure perching places among the vines to preen their feathers after bathing. Hummingbirds and mockingbirds like to perch on trellises, regardless of what vine is growing there, because they can get the high vantage point that these feisty, territorial birds desire.

Train fast-growing moonflower up a trellis and you'll have a lush (and safe) roosting place for the birds.

PERENNIAL VINES

Many types of perennial vines offer food and shelter for birds. And unlike annual vines, which die away each fall, perennial vines grow bigger and better every year.

Plant perennial vines in spring, starting with potted plants to get a head start. Choose your vines according to the conditions of your yard: Some thrive in shade, while others flourish in full sun. All will grow well in average, well-drained soil. Perennial vines start out slowly, but during their second or third growing season, they may zoom to incredible lengths. They're easy to keep in bounds, though, with a haircut every now and then. Pruning perennial vines is easiest in winter, after the vine has dropped its leaves and you can easily see the branch structure. You can keep established plants in bounds by snipping them back with pruners at any time of year if they stray from their supporting trellis.

Don't be shy about cutting back a perennial vine; these hardy specimens will quickly recover from even a drastic pruning session. Usually, nipping back side branches is all the pruning you'll need to do. But you can even cut a mature vine to the ground and expect vigorous regrowth.

CLEMATIS

Plant a trellis or fence near your feeders with sweet autumn clematis (*C. terniflora,* also called *C. maximowicziana*) or other small-flowered types such as anemone clematis (*C. montana*) or virginsbower (*C. virginiana*), and your birds will have plenty of reasons to thank you.

These vigorous, twiggy vines provide excellent shelter from rain or wind for any bird, and the vine is a great place to hide in a hurry should a hawk dive-bomb the feeders. The multitude of tiny flowers are better at attracting insects than those large, colorful hybrid clematis blooms. Birds will visit the flowering vines to snap up small flies, wasps, and other tasty insects.

In fall, when seedheads mature, cardinals, finches, juncos, and sparrows will work busily to tear away the fluff and get at seeds. In spring, sparrows and other songbirds will tug off pieces of bare clematis vine to use in building their nests.

Small-flowered clematis are speedy growers that thrive in sun to full shade and are perfect for quick coverage of a fence, wall, or trellis. These trouble-free vines never need fertilizer and require no additional watering after their first few weeks in the ground. Most clematis grow well in Zones 3 through 8.

HONEYSUCKLE

From a bird's-eye point of view, honeysuckles are real winners. Catbirds, cardinals, song sparrows, and other birds nest in the tangled vines. Honeysuckles produce bold clusters of tubular, nectar-rich blossoms that draw hummingbirds and orioles. And the blue-black berries are a favorite snack of robins, waxwings, chickadees, and many other birds.

But from a gardener's viewpoint, honeysuckle can be a thug. Some honeysuckle vines spread rampantly. Birds contribute by sowing the seeds far and wide. So choose honeysuckles with care, and plant them where they won't choke out less vigorous plants.

Trumpet or coral honeysuckle (*Lonicera sempervirens*), native to the East and South, and Arizona honeysuckle (*L. arizonica*), a Southwest plant, both have orange-red flowers and bright red berries. The vivid flowers attract hummingbirds.

Trumpet honeysuckle (Zones 4 to 9) is evergreen in the South and semievergreen in colder regions. This native of woods and shady

Growing Honeysuckles

HONEYSUCKLES are ideal for disguising unsightly fences and outbuildings. Honeysuckle vines can reach heights of 30 feet with support. They're as happy scrambling over shrubs and dead or fallen trees as they are climbing a trellis, and many grow as well in filtered shade as they do in sun. When your honeysuckle vines get too rambunctious, just cut them back as drastically as you need to—you won't harm the plants. But wait to prune until the vines finish blooming so you don't deprive the birds of their beautiful, nectar-filled flowers.

roadside thickets does well in both sun and shade. Arizona honey-suckle is deciduous and grows best in full sun.

And the heady fragrance of Japanese honeysuckle (*L. japonica*) on a summer night has inspired many gardeners to add this vine to their garden, where it is indeed a delight.

MORNING GLORIES

Morning glory vines are great for providing quick covers for birds near a feeding station. The vines grow thick and fast, making a tangle where birds can easily take refuge. A trellis of morning glories is just the thing to shelter your feeders from hot summer winds

Support Systems

MOST vines grow best with a support like a fence or arbor. Unless you have a carpenter in the family, it's easiest to buy a ready-made trellis or arbor that you can easily put up in a couple of hours or less. Garden centers have finished trellises and arbors that will do the job. But choose carefully: Some premade trellises will last only a year or two in the garden. For a long-lasting trellis or arbor that's strong enough to hold a heavy vine, shop for one with thick corner posts and crosspieces that are firmly attached with nails—or better yet, screws.

Lattice panels are too delicate to hold up heavy perennial vines, but they make excellent supports for lightweight annual vines. Edging the panels by sandwiching them between thicker boards will make them stronger and more finished looking. If you want to put lattice against a wall, frame the panels with 1 × 4s. If you want the panels to be strong enough to stand by themselves, frame them with 2 × 4s, making the vertical end pieces long enough to set into the ground.

If you're growing vines against a wall or solid wood fence, attach sections of wire fencing or chicken wire to it to support the vines. The stems of the vines will twine around the wires, and in no time the foliage will hide all traces of the wire.

and to give feeder birds a quick hideaway when danger threatens. A trellis of morning glories is terrific next to a birdbath, too, because the trellis gives wet-feathered birds a safe place to preen.

Fast-growing annual morning glory (*Ipomoea tricolor*) can brighten a garden just about anywhere. Choose a sunny garden spot for your trellis, and plant the seeds next to it in spring after danger of frost is past. If summers are short in your area, start the seeds indoors about 3 weeks before the last spring frost date. Otherwise, the vines may not have time to produce flowers before fall frost kills them. Morning glories grow well in containers, too, so you can let them wrap around an upper deck railing or twine along a first-floor window frame.

Hardy morning glories are even better than annual morning glories for providing cover for birds. "Man-of-the-earth" (*I. pandurata*) thrives through Zone 6. Its white flowers are splashed with red-purple middles and look like any pretty morning glory, but below the earth, this perennial vine grows enormous tubers.

Large morning glory flowers may tempt a passing hummingbird, but for continual hummer traffic, plant one of the small-flowered red species. Cypress vine (*I. quamoclit*) is a delicate climber with soft, feathery leaves that look like the foliage of cypress or dawn redwood. Let it ramble about the perennials in your beds, or grow it on a trellis. Red star morning glory (*I. coccinea*), with thick, heart-shaped foliage, is a more vigorous plant that grows best on a trellis or fence. Both will buzz with hummingbirds all summer long.

TRUMPET VINES

Trumpet vines shine like a beacon to hummingbirds. When in bloom in mid- through late summer, its trumpet-shaped flowers are constantly buzzing with hummers. The orange, red, or yellow flowers and lush foliage of trumpet vine make a dazzling sight sprawling on a trellis or arbor.

Hardy from Zones 4 to 9, trumpet vine (*Campsis radicans*) will grow in rich soil or sun-baked clay and just about everywhere in between. Trumpet vine blooms best in full sun but also puts on a decent show in the shade.

Totally untroubled by pests or disease, trumpet vine can climb as high as 30 feet, but you can keep it short and shrubby by pruning. Don't be timid with this vine: You can prune it to the ground in early spring and it will be up and blooming by late summer. Wear gloves and long sleeves when you work because all parts of the plant can irritate your skin.

Trumpet vine is a strong, heavy vine that clings to supports with rootlike growths called holdfasts along its stems. If you build an arbor or a trellis for trumpet vines,

use sturdy 4 × 4 posts and 2 × 4 crosspieces because the weight of a mature vine will pull down anything flimsier in a few years. Promptly pull out any volunteer seedlings or suckers that sprout from underground runners.

VIRGINIA CREEPER

When you find a Virginia creeper vine in fruit, you're bound to find titmice, chickadees, vireos, grosbeaks, and many other fruit-eating birds snapping up the plentiful blue berries. Downy woodpeckers are especially fond of

Vining Vegetables

BECAUSE cover and insects are what attract birds to vines (plus any edible fruit), some of the plants you relegate to the vegetable garden are worth considering in other areas. For example, vining squash, melons, and pumpkins make a good, quick fence cover—and you can serve the seeds to birds and squirrels later. You can even grow cherry tomatoes as a vine—just keep tying the stems to a fence or trellis as they grow. The plump tomato hornworms that occasionally plague the plants are a fine snack for catbirds, wrens, and other garden friends. Birdhouse gourds display beautiful white flowers when in bloom and offer protective cover once the flowers are past their prime.

Virginia creeper berries, as are bluebirds, and quail will eagerly search out any berries that drop off the vines.

Virginia creeper (*Parthenocissus quinquefolia*) will bring beauty as well as birds to your garden. In the early fall, its leaves turn a glorious shade of crimson, and the deep blue berries cluster along bright red stems, making a wonderful contrast to the leaves.

Virginia creeper grows in Zones 3 to 9, in full sun to full shade, and in ordinary garden soil. The vines have suction-cup-like structures called holdfasts that will stick to a trellis or other support. These rambling vines can grow 10 feet or more in a single season. Choose a planting site carefully because it's hard to transplant Virginia creeper successfully. The easiest way to start new plants is to root cuttings taken in late summer.

OFF-SEASON VINE CARE

Birds still find vines useful even after the stems are dead or the leaves have dropped because they provide shelter and places to perch.

> **Plant a rambling Virginia creeper vine where it can cover a fence, wall, or sturdy trellis. Downy woodpeckers and bluebirds will flock to the vine in fall to devour its blue berries.**

A chain-link fence covered in morning glories, for instance, has value even in winter, when the vines have dried to tan, twisting stems. Sparrows and other birds often use the remains of annual vines as a place to gather on fall and winter days, and the branches of honeysuckle or other perennial vines may host a congregation of birds and even shelter them at night. Another advantage to letting annual vines stand is that they will drop their seeds, giving you a fresh crop of volunteers next season without you having to spend a penny. Of course, if you prefer a tidier look to your yard, you can cut back your annual vines at the end of the growing season (add the cuttings to your compost pile) and replant new ones next year.

For the most benefit to birds, let perennial vines stand all winter as a roosting haven and windbreak. Prune them back into shape if desired in very early spring. Nearly all perennial vines bloom on new wood—that is, stems that sprout from older branches in spring—so you won't have to worry about snipping off next season's flowers when you prune. Consider how severely grapevines in vineyards are routinely pruned—allowing only a few short branches on the main stem of the vine—and you'll see that vines are forgiving plants.

Even if you should sacrifice flowers, the vines will still attract birds with their abundant insect-hiding foliage and sheltering stems.

Reduce maintenance chores for trellises and arbors by using supports made of wood that can weather naturally, or weather-resistant metal or PVC. Plastic trellises and arbors continue to improve from the early days when they looked flimsy and fake. Many of today's plastic structures are almost indistinguishable from classic painted wood, and they come in plain or fancy styles.

Vines for Hummers

VINES with vivid red or orange flowers will bring hummingbirds to your garden. Transform a trellis with the miniature red trumpets of red morning glory (*Ipomoea coccinea*), cover a deck railing with annual scarlet runner beans (*Phaseolus coccineus*), or encourage the lacy-leaved cypress vine to wander throughout your garden. All are easy to grow in average garden soil in full sun.

In mild-winter areas create a bower with Chilean glory flower (*Eccremocarpus scaber*), a flame-flowered vine that will overwinter in Zones 9 and 10. In colder areas, you can start seeds of tender perennial vines like this indoors in early spring for bloom in summer.

Another vine with hummingbird appeal is orange-red or orange-flowered trumpet vine or bignonia (*Bignonia capreolata*), a trumpet-vine relative with appealing leaves that deepen to maroon after frost. Bignonia retains some of its leaves through the winter and is hardy in Zones 6 to 10.

Native Plants

NATIVE plants are a natural choice for bird-friendly gardens. When you grow native plants, birds know when the fruits or seeds will ripen, which plants have stems or leaves that make good nesting material, and which plants offer thorny branches or other protection for roosting and nests.

You'll love the beauty of native plants, too, like the spiky blooms of red cardinal flower (*Lobelia cardinalis*), which are sure to draw hummingbirds. Winterberry holly (*Ilex verticillata*) is a wonderful shrub for a foundation planting, and its bright red berries will draw waxwings, thrushes, and bluebirds to your garden in the fall.

Native plants that are adapted to your region and your local conditions are easy to grow and need no coddling. Besides being suited to your particular climate, native plants have evolved their own defenses to most insects and diseases.

The secret to success in choosing native plants is to realize that there's a big difference between being native to North America and being native to your area. Plant a California native in Pennsylvania and it may thrive if it's an adaptable plant, but it's no more "native" in your area than a plant from the Himalayas.

To choose appropriate native plants, go on some field trips in your area. Take a field guide along so you can identify plants that appeal to you. Jot down which trees grow with which shrubs, what wildflowers grow with which grasses. Imitate these wild plant groupings for a natural look and a successful garden.

If your garden is sunny, look for plants that thrive in nearby meadows, fields, deserts, or other bright places. If your home place is shady, look for plants of the woods. If your land is wet, check boggy areas and other low places.

Your well-chosen native plants will thrive with little or no care from you (beyond initial watering while they establish new roots). Before long, your garden will be as appealing—to you and the birds—as your favorite natural retreats. (For a list of favorite native plants for birds, see page 186.)

Grasses and Groundcovers

BIRDS would have a hard time getting along without grasses. Grass plants shelter nests, grass seeds sustain birds through fall and winter, and dry grass leaves are the perfect material for nest construction. Grasses also offer birds plenty of insect delicacies, from grasshoppers and crickets to aphids.

Groundcovers offer cover for ground-dwelling birds, and many of them bear bright fruits or flowers that attract hummingbirds, sparrows, towhees, and other birds. These spreading plants also keep your bird-friendly backyard looking tidy. When fruits and seed pods drop from trees and shrubs, they'll disappear into the camouflaging foliage of the groundcovers (but the hungry birds will still be able to find them).

Native species of grass, such as switchgrass, produce abundant seeds and supply nesting material and good cover.

GARDENING WITH GRASSES

Grasses are simple to grow. Most of them need full sun, although a few, like purple-top (*Tridens flavus*) and northen sea oats (*Chasmanthium latifolim*), flourish in shade. Most grow well in average, well-drained soil and usually need no fertilizer or watering. Many have long-lasting foliage that bleaches to a creamy white in fall and stays attractive throughout the winter. The only maintenance most ornamental grasses require is a yearly trimming with pruners or a string trimmer in early spring to cut off dead foliage.

When you plant ornamental grasses in your yard, think big. For example, cover a slope with a mix of grasses of different sizes to give birds plenty of elbowroom for collecting nesting materials and seeds. Try adding short grasses under shade trees to give cover to ground-feeding birds.

Grasses and shrubs make great combinations for beauty and for birds. In fall, the soft tans and golds of grasses are stunning against the flaming red leaves of bushy sumacs. And adding ornamental grasses to flowerbeds will give birds yet another place to feed and nest. Even after your perennials die back in winter, the seedheads of the dried grasses will continue to attract birds. (For specifics on the best grasses for birds, see page 189.)

GROUNDCOVERS

Instead of feeling like a Saturday morning slave to your lawn mower, fill the spaces of your backyard with groundcovers.

Besides saving labor and befriending birds, groundcovers also are great landscape plants. You can use a groundcover like periwinkle or cotoneaster to tie together isolated trees and shrubs for a more finished look.

You can choose from evergreen or deciduous groundcovers. Evergreen groundcovers are undemanding, hardy, and beautiful. Most grow from Zone 5 and colder regions to warm areas up to Zone 9. They grow in well-drained soils

ESTABLISHING GROUNDCOVERS at a glance

When you're ready to plant groundcovers, buy vigorous young plants—they'll spread faster than older plants. Then:

1. Clear grass and unwanted plants from the site.

2. Mulch with 4 inches of shredded bark, wood chips, gravel, or chopped leaves.

3. Pull back the mulch and make planting holes with a trowel for each plant.

4. Set plants at the same depth they occupied in the nursery pots.

5. Pull any tree seedlings that crop up by hand, before they get big enough to get a roothold.

with moderate rainfall and no fertilizer, in full sun to part shade. Evergreen groundcovers are favorites of the birds because the dense, waxy foliage sheds rain and winter snow and their berries arrive at the end of summer when other bird foods dwindle.

The leaves of deciduous groundcovers, like wild strawberries, die in winter. Even so, deciduous groundcovers retain some stems, branches, and dried leaves in winter, which can provide winter cover for birds. And by the time the plants make their reappearance in spring, you'll welcome the fresh greenery to hide the winter debris. For more on both evergreen and deciduous groundcovers, see "Groundcovers for Birds" on the opposite page.

Red lingonberries make a tasty treat for many birds, including cedar waxwings.

Groundcovers for Birds

BIRDS that forage for food at ground level, such as thrashers, catbirds, mockingbirds, waxwings, and robins, love a yard that includes groundcovers. Here's a look at seven bird-friendly ones.

Bearberry. The small shiny leaves of bearberry (*Arctostaphylos uva-ursi*) covers its mat of woody stems. Bearberry, an evergreen, thrives in Zones 2 to 6, and in Zones 7 and 8 in shade.

Cotoneaster. For a fast-growing groundcover that looks good all year, try cotoneaster (*Cotoneaster dammeri, C. horizontalis, C. adpressus,* and others). Its glossy, dark green leaves are dotted with red berries from fall into winter in Zones 4 to 8, depending on the species and cultivar.

Juniper. Junipers are tough, adaptable evergreens that provide excellent nesting sites and winter shelter for birds, as well as food in the form of juniper berries. Most junipers grow from Zones 3 to 9. Creeping juniper (*Juniperus horizontalis*) is a favorite nesting site for sparrows and juncos.

Lingonberry. This creeping evergreen shrub has pink urn-shaped flowers, small oval leaves, and red berries. Hummingbirds visit the flowers. Grow ligonberry (*Vaccinium vitis-idaea* var. *minus*) in full sun, in well-drained, moist acid soil high in organic matter. It's hardy in Zones 2 to 5.

Prickly pear. The spiny jointed pads of prickly pears (*Opuntia* spp.) can be as big around and as flat as dinner plates. These evergreen cacti have yellow flowers and egg-shaped red or yellow fruits favored by many birds. Grow prickly pears in full sun and in fertile, well-drained soil. Prickly pears grow throughout Zones 6 to 9.

Running serviceberry. In early spring, running serviceberry (*Amelanchier stolonifera*) forms dense thickets of erect stems about 4 feet tall. It produces white flowers that attract insects, which in turn attract insect-eating birds. The purple-black berries are also a bird favorite. Grow running serviceberry in either sun or shade, in Zones 4 to 9.

Strawberry. The small red fruits of wild strawberry (*Fragaria virginiana*) and beach strawberry (*F. chiloensis*) are favorites with many birds. Grow these mat-forming perennials in full sun and well-drained fertile soil in Zones 4 to 9.

Trees and Shrubs

TREES provide all kinds of food for birds, from acorns to seedpods to berries, plus countless insects. Trees also offer a safe place for birds to roost and build nests. In return, birds keep trees healthy and thriving by chowing down on aphids, caterpillars, bark beetles, and other pests that would otherwise reduce your backyard trees to a pile of sawdust.

BEST TREES FOR BIRDS

You can make the most of limited yard space by choosing trees that offer birds berries or nuts as well as shelter. Here's a sampling of some excellent choices to add to your landscape.

Cornelian cherry. A spreading tree or shrub of 20 to 25 feet tall, cornelian cherry (*Cornus mas*) is an early bloomer. Its yellow flowers are followed by red, oblong, bird-attracting fruits in summer. Grow cornelian cherry in well-drained, fertile soil, in sun to partial shade, in Zones 4 to 8.

White fringe tree. White fringe tree (*Chionanthus virginicus*) is a small tree that grows from 12 to 20 feet tall. Its lacy, fragrant, white flower heads are followed by grapelike clusters of blue berries that birds adore. Grow white fringe tree in moist, fertile soil, in full sun, in Zones 3 to 9.

Black gum. The elegant black gum (*Nyssa sylvatica*) is usually 30 to 40 feet tall, with drooping branches, bluish black fruits, and oval leaves that turn an attractive scarlet in fall. Grow it in moist, well-drained, acidic soil, in sun or shade, in Zones 3 to 9.

Hawthorn. Thorny-branched hawthorns (*Crataegus* spp.) grow 15 to 25 feet tall. Their clouds of small, creamy white flowers and beautiful, glowing berries hold great appeal to birds. The long thorns can be hazardous, so don't plant hawthorns if small children (yours or your neighbor's) play in your yard. Grow hawthorn in well-drained soil, in full sun, in Zones 3 to 7.

Eastern redbud. Fast-growing and trouble-free eastern redbud (*Cercis canadensis*) is a 20-foot-tall American native that's flushed with pinkish purple flowers in early spring. The flowers attract insects, which then attract migrating wood warblers. Flat, dark brown seedpods keep chickadees and titmice happy in winter. Grow redbud in well-drained soil in full sun to light shade, in Zones 4 to 9.

Downy serviceberry. A graceful, often multistemmed, small tree, downy serviceberry (*Amelanchier arborea*) grows 25 feet tall and has white flowers in early spring. Its bird-attracting berries turn from green to red, and finally to purplish black. The leaves turn a fine shade of red in fall. Grow downy serviceberry in moist, well-drained acid soil, in full sun to partial shade, in Zones 3 to 8.

Sassafras. Sassafras (*Sassafras albidum*) is a handsome shade tree that grows to 30 feet tall or taller. Its large leaves turn brilliant gold to flaming orange in fall. Birds will eat the dark blue fruits as soon as they ripen in fall. Grow sassafras in moist, well-drained, acid soil, in full sun to light shade, in Zones 4 to 9.

Tulip poplar. If you have space for a large shade tree, consider planting tulip poplar (*Liriodendron tulipifera*), which can reach 100 feet tall. It has pointed, lobed leaves and

Beautiful Bayberries

BAYBERRY (*Myrica pensylvanica*) is a beauty in the garden, thanks to its glossy narrow leaves and waxy blue-gray berries, which remain on the shrub through the winter. Yellow-rumped warblers, bluebirds, and other birds may feast on a backyard bayberry's fruits.

Bayberries may be shrubby or grow into a small tree up to 9 feet tall. They thrive in any soil unless it's alkaline, need no fertilizing, tolerate drought, and grow well in Zones 2 to 7. Be sure to plant a male shrub along with your female shrubs for best fruit production.

sweet-smelling flowers, with creamy, waxy petals and a green-and-orange central blotch. Flowers mature into pineconelike seedpods, which attract goldfinches, pine siskins, purple finches, cardinals, and evening grosbeaks throughout the winter. Grow tulip poplar in deep, moist, well-drained soil, in full sun, in Zones 4 to 9.

SHRUBS

Shrubs are ideal places for birds to nest, sleep, and hide from predators and bad weather. Shrubs are also a delicatessen of bird delights.

Birds will scour your shrubs in all seasons looking for insects, egg masses, or cocoons hidden among the branches or dangling from twigs. The leaf litter beneath your shrubs is a happy hunting ground for sparrows, thrushes, grackles, and other birds who scratch or sift through the leaves and humus to find tasty insects. The flowers of shrubs attract yet more insects, and their fruits and berries add the crowning touch.

Plus, shrubs are so vital to birds that you could plant nothing but shrubs and still attract more birds than you could with a yard full of

Viburnums

VIBURNUMS are a diverse group of shrubs and small trees—there are more than 150 different kinds. They bear plentiful blooms and some have fall foliage that's as brilliant as a sugar maple. Berries are the biggest bird draw that a viburnum offers. The berries come in red, blue, and orange; robins, thrashers, waxwings, and other berry-eating birds love them.

Viburnum foliage is dense, making the shrubs a protected location where birds can search for insects or hide nests. Cardinals, catbirds, and sparrows all like to nest in viburnums. These shrubs are fast-growing, too, so they're a fine choice for a hedge or shrub grouping to provide the cover that makes your yard more appealing to birds in general. A mixed group of viburnums staggers the berry-ripening schedule, so birds don't clean off all the bushes in one fell swoop.

trees and flowers. Shrubs like barberries and burning bush provide safe cover for foraging for food and nesting materials. The twiggy branches and dense foliage shield birds from predators like hawks, which can't get into the dense interiors of the bushes. If your yard is thickly planted with shrubs, birds will feel at ease there and move about freely.

Shrubs with dense, overlapping foliage shelter birds from wind and rain, and shrubs of all kinds also offer a cool respite of shade. The twiggy, sheltered interior of a shrub is a perfect spot for a nest. Birds that spend most of their time on or near the ground, including song sparrows and other native sparrows, buntings, and thrushes, often build nests in backyard shrubs. Shrubs also offer a jackpot of nesting materials like dead twigs and leaves.

Fruiting shrubs like viburnums are the best bird magnet there is. The birds they attract are often unusual beauties—bluebirds, waxwings, grosbeaks, and others. But it's not only berries that provide food for birds. Flowering shrubs provide nectar for hummingbirds.

Blossoms and leaves attract tiny insects, which in turn attract warblers, vireos, and other bug eaters. When songbirds are feeding nestlings, a garden full of shrubs is as popular as a fast-food restaurant.

Shrubs are great garden bargains. They're inexpensive to buy, costing as little as a few dollars. They grow fast and live practically forever. Rarely troubled by disease or severe insect outbreaks, shrubs just keep growing year after year, providing the garden with permanent color and structure.

Shrubs are generally easy to establish in your yard. They put out new roots quickly and begin sprouting healthy new growth even in their first season. There's no need to fertilize, but be sure to water shrubs when rain is scarce during their first year, especially in late fall when they need a good drink to get them through winter.

While a single shrub will attract birds, a group of shrubs has much more appeal. There's safety in numbers, and a grouping, hedge, or corridor of shrubs helps birds feel more secure. When birds are less nervous about predators, they're much more likely to linger in your backyard.

Plants

Cosmos Impatiens Sunflowers Zinnias Bee balm Columbine Fuchsias Vines Trees Shrubs

Berries

IF you don't already have a berry-producing plant in your yard, you should add one—you'll be amazed at the number of new names you'll be adding to the checklist of birds that pop in for a bite to eat. Berries attract a slew of birds, including gorgeous bright-colored tanagers, orioles, and grosbeaks.

Blueberries aren't really that hard to grow—and their sweet fruit will entice all kinds of feathered friends.

BLUEBERRIES

When blueberry fruits begin to ripen, birds descend on the berry patch and gobble up berry after berry until their bellies are so full they can barely fly.

If you've never tried growing blueberries, don't let the "finicky blueberry" reputation scare you off. If you can grow hollies (*Ilex* spp.), azaleas (*Rhododendron* spp.), or rhododendrons (*Rhododendron* spp.), you can grow blueberries. These American natives are well known for liking acid soil, a condition that's usually not hard to meet. Unless you live near a limestone outcrop or in one of the alkaline areas of the West, your soil should be reasonably close to blueberry range. A do-it-yourself soil test will give you the information you need. But if the azaleas in your yard are thriving, you can skip that step and go ahead and plant your berry bushes. An annual mulch of chopped oak leaves, cypress bark, beech leaves, or other acidic material will help keep your soil pH in the range that's just right for blueberry plants.

(Of course, if the berries that catbird is gobbling are the ones you intended for your blueberry cobbler, you may feel a certain conflict of interest. Once a blueberry patch is established and growing for a few years, it produces enough berries for you and the birds to share. But when your berries are new and small, you may want to throw a sheet of plastic bird netting over the patch to protect your crop.)

BRAMBLES

A patch of blackberries, raspberries, or other "bramble" fruits in your yard attracts fun-loving birds like thrushes and wrens, and many birds will nest in brambles. When choosing brambles, stick with disease-resistant cultivars (if they're available) and plant the brambles on a site with the soil and light conditions that suit them best.

Blackberries (*Rubus* spp.) range in form from erect cultivars like 'Comanche' to trailing ones like 'Cascade' to American dewberry (*R. flagellaris*), which makes a perfect groundcover. Blackberries have vicious thorns, but the thorns protect roosting and nesting birds. Thornless cultivars, such as 'Navaho', attract birds with their bounty of delectable fruit.

Blackberry hybrids also produce solid berries with firm cores. The hybrids are less hardy than

Growing Brambles

IF you're planting raspberries or blackberries, start with certified virus-free, bareroot plants from a garden center or catalog. Look for unusual species at native-plant nurseries or in specialty mail-order catalogs. Most brambles are hardy enough to grow in Zones 5 to 9.

Plant bramble plants 3 feet or more apart in a moist, sunny spot. Wineberries grow better in shade or partial shade. Bramble canes won't fruit the first year. In the second year they'll flower, fruit, and die. However, new canes sprout from the crowns each year. The varieties called everbearing, like 'Heritage' red raspberry, will produce a few berries in their first year of growth.

regular blackberries, most growing only in Zones 8 and 9. Loganberries have big, light red berries with a slightly tart taste. Marionberries have a mild flavor. Boysenberries bear huge, maroon berries brimming with juice. Tayberries (a cross between blackberries and black raspberries) have a strong, complex flavor.

Black raspberries (*R. occidentalis*) are so delicious that no backyard should be without them. As with blackberries, some cultivars are thornless.

If you plant brambles—such as raspberries—for the birds, make sure you buy certified virus-free plants.

Red raspberries (*R. idaeus*) have a milder, sweeter flavor than black raspberries. Summerbearing and everbearing cultivars are available. 'Latham' is a summerbearer; 'Heritage' is an everbearer that gives both a summer crop and a heavier fall crop.

Wineberries (*R. phoenicolasius*) bear tangy-sweet red fruits. The trouble-free mounded plants with arching canes flourish in moist soils and partial shade. Though the canes are prickly to touch, they're beautiful to look at in winter, especially when you grow the plants next to ornamental grasses.

MULBERRIES

Flashy-colored fruit eaters like orioles, tanagers, grosbeaks, thrashers, great crested flycatchers, and bluebirds love to stuff themselves on the soft, blackberry-shaped fruits of mulberries. Mulberries also attract flycatchers, vireos, warblers, thrushes, and waxwings. In fact, just about every songbird in the area will search out a mulberry tree when the juicy berries ripen in early summer.

Mulberry fruit can be messy, but the trees draw so many birds in such incredible quantities that it's worth a bit of creative planning to find a place for a mulberry tree in your yard. Pick a site away from walks and driveways, and surround the tree with a thick ground-cover like pachysandra so that fallen fruit "disappears"—and you won't have to worry about cleaning it up. If your yard is small and doesn't have an appropriate isolated spot, try planting a white-fruited cultivar of white mulberry (*Morus alba*). The white berries are just as big a draw for birds, and they won't leave telltale stains on cars or your line-dried laundry.

Mulberries are hardy trees untroubled by the pests and diseases that affect other fruit-bearing trees. They'll grow in any sunny spot in any type of soil, as long as it's well-drained. Seedlings can sprout like weeds, so keep an eye out for volunteers "planted" by birds and pull them out while they're small.

Mulberry fruits aren't just for the birds. They're sweet and tasty for humans to eat, too. If you'd like to harvest some for yourself, spread a clean cloth on the ground below the tree, and gently shake branches to make the fruits drop. If you plant to make jam or pies, harvest the fruit when it's slightly underripe.

Mulberry Choices

PURPLE-FRUITED red mulberry (*Morus rubra*) is the giant of the mulberry trees, reaching 60 feet tall. Black mulberry (*M. nigra*) is a small, spreading tree of about 20 feet tall that becomes wonderfully gnarled with age. Both thrive in Zones 5 to 8.

Whilte mulberry (*M. alba*) can have white, pink, or purple fruits, so read plant tags and catalog descriptions carefully when buying. It grows to 60 feet tall and flourishes in Zones 4 to 8.

Mulberries have separate male and female trees, but some female trees will set fruit even if the flowers aren't pollinated. Ask when you buy whether the tree will need a pollinator.

STRAWBERRIES

Those juicy red fruits of strawberries are incredibly tempting for birds. So use that appeal to lure fruit-eating birds, such as catbirds, mockingbirds, robins, and thrashers, by planting strawberries (*Fragaria* spp.) wherever you can squeeze them in: Use them as an edging along a driveway or walkway, as groundcover around a birdbath, or as a border at the front of your flowerbeds.

Birds aren't particular about what variety of strawberry you plant. Their sharp beaks can easily nip a slice out of even the biggest strawberry, while small wild (*F. vesca*) or alpine strawberries (*F. montana fraga*) go down the hatch whole. Select a variety that thrives in your area and is disease-resistant. Or locate native wild strawberries at a specialty nursery. Order your strawberry plants early from a catalog for the best selection of your favorite varieties. Plant the bareroot plants as soon as they arrive in spring, following the directions included in the package. Or buy plants in early spring at local nurseries; they are usually sold in bareroot bundles. Plant so that the growing tip of the plant, from which the leaves will emerge, is above ground. After the ground freezes in the fall, cover your strawberry bed with several inches of hay or straw mulch for winter protection. Remove the mulch in the spring before the plants begin to grow. Strawberry plants send out runners from the parent plant in subsequent seasons. Expand your planting by slicing off the plantlets at the ends of the runners and transplanting them.

Alpine strawberries serve double duty as both an attractive groundcover and an easy meal for the birds.

Creating a Green Scene

Q I want to encourage birds to visit my vegetable garden because I'm hoping they'll help keep the pest insects under control. How can I invite them in?

A Because your frequent presence in the garden is a deterrent to birds, it's important to sweeten the deal to get birds to overcome their initial hesitation. Try placing a pedestal birdbath among the plots and keep it brimming with fresh water. Mount nest boxes for bluebirds and wrens in and around the garden. Entice birds with a sour cherry tree at one side of the garden. After they feast on fruit, they'll move to the vegetables to hunt for insects. If you can, visit your garden at regular times. Birds will learn your schedule and visit when you're not there.

Q I'd like to plant some trees or shrubs specifically for the birds, but I don't have unlimited space. Any advice on what would offer the most benefits to birds?

A Hollies have it all, as far as birds are concerned. Their red, yellow, or black berries fill many a hungry bird's belly in fall and winter. Prickly holly leaves offer birds protection from climbing cats and other predators, and the dense foliage hides nests and sheds rain and snow like tiny umbrellas.

Most hollies grow well in Zones 5 to 8. They set fruit in full sun to light shade but do best when grown in deep, moist, well-drained soil. Keep in mind that hollies are male and female—each type of plant bears only male or female flowers. To get female hollies to bear heavy fruit, plant one male holly as a pollinator for every three females.

Fruit Trees

FRUIT trees are for the birds, as many a dismayed backyard orchardist has discovered. When cherries, peaches, or other fruits swell to juicy perfection, birds are often on the scene before you are—almost as if they've been watching from a distance, waiting for the big day. If a bountiful harvest is your main reason for having fruit trees, then you'll need to protect the fruit with netting or bird-scare devices. But if attracting birds is your goal, pull up a chair and enjoy the show.

Disease Prevention at a glance

Three important techniques help prevent diseases from occurring in fruit trees.

- Apply dormant oil in late winter to smother insect larvae.
- Clean up dropped leaves and fruits in fall to remove the overwintering places of insects and diseases.
- Prune out dead or diseased branches.

Choosing Fruit Trees

Crabapple trees and some cultivars of apples are a good choice for birds because the fruits hang on the branches well into winter. You'll notice that the fruits continue to attract birds no matter how shriveled and unappealing they look to us.

With today's modern dwarf varieties of cherries, apples, plums, and other fruits, there's no need to relegate these bird-beloved plants to a separate "orchard" section of your yard. Let a dwarf apricot tree add a drift of white blossoms to your perennial garden, plant a thorny hedgerow of beach plums for privacy, or accent your doorway with a dwarf apple tree. The idea is to keep the fruit trees up close, where you can watch the birds they bring.

When it comes to fruit trees, you have plenty of choices to make, even after you decide what kind of fruit you want to grow. Tree size, hardiness, disease resistance, and pollination requirements are some important factors to ponder when you select fruit trees for your yard.

For most backyard gardeners, dwarf fruit trees make the most sense. For example, a dwarf apple tree stays at a very manageable height of 8 to 12 feet, whereas an unpruned standard-size apple tree can stretch to 40 feet tall. Semi-dwarf apple trees grow to a height of about 20 feet tall.

You can grow all the familiar fruit trees—apples, pears, plums, cherries, apricots, and peaches—just about everywhere in the United States except for the hottest and coldest climates. Peaches and nectarines have the most restricted range, doing best in Zones 6 to 9, but many tree fruits are cold-hardy to Zone 2. Because climate and conditions can vary so widely across the country, you'll need to choose a cultivar that's suited to your area. Your local garden centers carry varieties that are suited to your own conditions; but if

Cherry Choices

IF you have a small yard, try planting common chokecherries (*Prunus virginiana*) or tart cherries (*P. cerasus*). Chokecherry (Zones 2 to 8) is a shrub or small tree that reaches 10 feet tall. In the spring it's covered with creamy, fragrant flowers and in summer, with tart or yellow fruits. Tart cherry, which is also called sour cherry, grows to 20 feet and sets tangy red fruits.

For a moderate-size tree that will also provide some shade, try sweet cherry (*P. avium*) or pin cherry (*P. pensylvanica*). Sweet cherry (Zones 3 to 9) grows to 35 feet tall and has large, sweet fruits that can be red, purple, or yellow. Unlike other types of cherries, sweet cherries require cross-pollination, so ask your supplier which cultivars to plant to ensure good fruiting. Pin cherry grows to 40 feet, and it produces clusters of sour red fruits.

plants

Cosmos Impatiens Sunflowers Zinnias Bee balm Columbine Fuchsias Vines Trees Shrubs

The addition of even one fruit tree to your backyard can increase the number of birds that stop by to visit.

you're selecting from a catalog, pay attention to the regional recommendations.

Fruit trees that bloom early in the spring, such as peaches and cherries, often fall victim to late cold snaps that freeze the swelling buds or blossoms, preventing fruit set. If spring weather is unsettled in your area, plant these trees on the north side of your house, where they'll be less prone to blooming early.

In many cases, fruit trees need a second tree growing nearby to pollinate their flowers. Sour cherries, peaches, and most apricots are exceptions—a single tree planted alone will bear loads of fruit. Many pears are self-fruitful but bear better with a pollinator.

5
FEEDING
THROUGH THE
SEASONS

Fare for Spring, Summer, Fall, and Winter

ALTHOUGH WINTER MONTHS are prime time for feeding birds, that doesn't mean birds don't appreciate a handout the rest of the year. In fact, if you want birds to become regulars in your backyard, you need to permanently put out the welcome mat at your feeders. Of course, you'll need to adjust what you're serving depending on the season, but if you do, you're guaranteed to have a host of feathered friends to watch and delight in all year long.

Spring Almanac

BIRD watchers know that spring arrives long before the first robin makes its grand entrance. The new season is ushered in by owls, titmice, and chickadees, whose fancies turn to love even before winter gives its final gasp. If you're lucky enough to have a patch of woods in your yard or nearby, start listening in late winter for the deep-throated booming hoots of great horned owls, which begin raising a family in February or even earlier.

Closer to home, tune your ear to the high-pitched whines of chickadees and titmice. The screechiness of these love calls makes some people cringe. Both titmice and chickadees have other love songs up their sleeves, and they start singing even before the first pussy willow breaks free of its brown shell.

COMINGS AND GOINGS

Although you won't notice much of a change in the number of birds at your feeders early in the season, you will see a change in behavior. Instead of congregating in congenial groups, many species are now beginning courtship maneuvers and forming pair bonds. Sparring over females is common, and territorial jousting can occur between males of the same species.

Feeder birds sound different in spring, too. Their hormone levels are changing, triggering them to begin singing their love songs. Blackbirds, bluebirds, chickadees, meadowlarks, nuthatches, song sparrows, starlings, and titmice are among the first to start singing. Watch them to see whether they're trying to impress a mate or stake out a territory. By midspring, courtship manuevers are happening everywhere you look. Watch for the mourning doves that nibbled millet all winter at the feeder to begin billing and cooing—with head bobbing and bowing—it can go on for hours. Birds that once shared the yard and feeders in friendly groups, like cardinals, jays, and chickadees, turn territorial in spring as they claim nesting areas. Look for skirmishes as male birds chase each other from their own territories.

Arriving spring migrants are cause for big excitement at the feeders because now is the time when some of the most colorful, most unusual birds may show up. Insects are still scarce, and the need to refuel quickly is paramount, which means that tanagers may choose an hour of feasting at your feeder over an afternoon of foraging for themselves.

If your feeders offer generous helpings of favored foods, you may find an ever-increasing number of birds as migrants come into the area and stop for a few days. Goldfinches, in particular, can build into enormous flocks at a well-stocked feeder.

Migration is usually gradual. Not every bird species has a departure ticket for the same day. As winter residents leave for more northerly breeding grounds, you won't need to fill your feeder as often as you had in the previous months.

As spring progresses and the birds move to nesting territories, their visits to your feeder will likely become fewer and farther between. By late spring, nesting season is in full swing, migration is over, and feeder traffic usually drops off dramatically. Don't worry, though: Some of the faithfuls will stay regular customers right through summer.

SPRING FEEDING
at a glance

Important to-dos for your feathered friends once spring arrives include:

■ Increase the amount of millet in your feeders to satisfy the many small seed eaters that may be stopping in, such as indigo buntings, finches, siskins, and native sparrows.

■ Add another tube feeder if needed to accommodate the burgeoning numbers of goldfinches.

■ Pull out special treats to keep birds loyal to your feeder: nuts, peanuts, fruits, and peanut-butter delicacies.

■ Offer crushed eggshells to replenish minerals.

■ Keep a ready supply of fresh water available to the birds.

AT THE FEEDER

Breakfast at the feeder window is always an adventure in spring. One day you may find a rose-breasted grosbeak, resplendent in snow white, shining black, and crimson breeding plumage, cracking sunflower seeds; the next morning, brilliant indigo buntings may sparkle in the sunlight.

You can do a bunch of things to help please your spring visitors. Put out the hummingbird feeder for early arrivals. Look for them when spring-blooming red flowers like wild columbine, flowering quince, or red-flowering currant begin to blossom. Stock up on soft foods for insect eaters that return in spring. Mealworms are a welcome treat for bluebirds. Suet is a favorite with many birds, including yellow-rumped warblers. Blackbirds, robins, and jays will appreciate bread.

Freshen up the area below your bird feeders with a 2-inch layer of bark mulch to cover the winter's accumulation of seed hulls. If a late snowstorm hits your area, stock up with bread, and head out in your car. Leave pieces of bread near hedgerows where robins are sheltering. Include some dark bread as well so it's easily visible from a distance or to a bird flying overhead. Robins and some other birds need soft foods, and the life-saving bread holds them over until the snow melts.

IN THE GARDEN

Of course, spring will find you planting annual flowers, which birds will enjoy in summer (be-cause of the insects) and fall (for the seeds). But there are other spring gardening activities that are fun for you and good for the birds.

■ Now's the time to add a garden bench—or a second one—so that you can sit in the thick of things with your morning cup of tea and your binoculars at the ready. Watch

for motion among the branches and stems, and don't forget to watch for secretive birds, like wood thrushes, fox sparrows, and towhees, that stay low to the ground in thick shrubbery.

■ Offer a reliable source of water in your garden—it's one of the best ways to attract birds. Spring is a good time to add a small pool, a bubbling spring, or another water feature.

In spring, tempt visitors such as tanagers to your feeders with special treats. They'll appreciate delicacies like peanut butter mixed with cornmeal—or chopped bananas.

■ Have a little fun with mud: Create a nice sloppy puddle for robins, swallows, and other birds to use in nest building. Make your puddle about 2 feet in diameter and 4 inches deep in the center; any smaller and it will dry out too quickly.

■ Don't plant just flowers. Berry bushes, evergreens, and other shrubs and trees for food and shelter top the list for a bird-friendly garden.

■ Drape short lengths of white string over your shrubs for orioles, and scatter white feathers, dog-hair combings, or other soft materials. Birds will pick them up to line a cozy nest.

■ Early spring is the time to put up more birdhouses or nesting shelves so there's plenty of prime real estate waiting and ready when wrens, phoebes, and woodpeckers are looking for a home.

Little Rain?

IN the arid Southwest and in other places such as the Northwest where rain is scarce or nonexistent for months at a time, birds have evolved to take advantage of water wherever they can find it. Morning dew is a treasured source of water but, like puddles and streams, dew also disappears when rain fails to fall and air and soil become parched. But the biggest sources of liquid refreshment for desert birds are succulent plant parts and living food. Fruits are eagerly sought for their thirst-satisfying juice as well as for their food value. Prickly pear, cholla, and barrel cactuses are good places to bird-watch when their colorful fruits ripen and lure quail and other birds to the feast. Other plant parts also contain water.

Where rain is scarce during a drought, a regular source of water is even more attractive to birds than the most carefully selected banquet at the feeder. Birdbaths and water features will have a steady stream of customers. To ensure room for all, place shallow clay saucers or other impromptu bird-baths at ground level throughout the yard so your birds can quench their thirst or freshen their feathers.

WET WEATHER

April showers may bring May flowers—but what's all that rain doing to the birds and their food?

You needn't worry. A little rain doesn't bother birds. During a rain shower, you'll see birds at your feeders, cracking seeds and nibbling suet, giving an occasional shake to flick water from their feathers.

When rain intensifies, or if there are gusty winds or lightning, birds wait out the storm in the shelter of densely branched trees and shrubs. To make sure birds will feel at home in your yard no matter what the weather, be sure they have a spot to take shelter from heavy rain. If your yard is very open, try planting a couple of bushy junipers (*Juniperus* spp.), camellias, hollies, rhododendrons, or other broad-leaved evergreens to provide some quick shelter.

At the feeder, especially tray feeders and hopper feeders, rain means wet seed. Check your feeders after the weather clears, and remove any wet seed so that it doesn't turn moldy or ruin new seed that you add. Suet and whole corncobs can stand up to rain; they will dry out without damage. If the wet weather is prolonged, however, even corncobs may rot, and tube feeders may accumulate moisture inside that causes seed to clump up and decay. You may need to compost the spoiled food and re-place it with fresh.

Always check your tray feeders after a rain and remove any wet food so it doesn't turn moldy.

Summer Almanac

EARLY summer is family time for backyard birds. Parent birds actively search all nooks and crannies of the garden for insect morsels to feed their constantly demanding babies. Soon nestlings make the leap to fledglings, flying on a learner's permit as they learn the fine points to handling their wings.

Mid- to late summer is a transition time as birds finish with raising families and migratory songbirds begin the changes and preparations needed for the long journey they face in the fall to their wintering range.

COMINGS AND GOINGS

The summer scene at the feeding station is sparse compared to the overflow crowds of fall and winter. With insects abundant and wild fruits ripening, birds don't need to depend on your generosity to satisfy their needs. Many species are nesting, too, which means they'll be spending most of their days in frantic search for insects rather than leisurely kibitzing among themselves at your backyard feeders.

Still, you'll find that some loyal customers remain regulars at your feeders throughout the dog days. Cardinals, chickadees, finches, grackles, jays, and other birds will drop in to grab a snack daily. And, for better or worse, house sparrows and starlings will never desert you.

The summer feeding season is the time to enjoy the fruits of your landscaping labors. Now the payoff of all that planting is at hand, as birds flock to your yard to find food in your shrubs, trees, and garden beds. They'll be looking for fruit and berries, but they'll also be patrolling for creeping, crawling food like caterpillars and beetles. This is a great time to watch birds acting naturally in your yard, as they gather food for nestlings.

AT THE FEEDER

Many feeder keepers take a break from stocking feed in the summer. Birds won't suffer if you stop feeding them in summer as

SUMMER FEEDING
at a glance

During the dog days of summer, make sure you:

- Monitor seed supplies for webbing, larvae, or other signs of insect infestation.

- Clean up hulls beneath feeders and replace mulch.

- Move suet feeders to the shade to slow melting.

- Replace beef-fat trimmings with processed suet blocks, which resist melting.

- Add an oriole nectar feeder for sweet-toothed songbirds.

- Freeze blueberries and other small fruits for winter feeding when the birds will really appreciate a sweet treat.

- Cut back on your feedings so that seed doesn't go to waste.

they would in winter, but you still might want to keep a few feeders stocked with fresh seed—for your own enjoyment as much as theirs. A tube feeder of niger and one or two hopper or tray feeders will accommodate the summer seed-eating guests. If you continue feeding the birds, cut down on the amount of seed you put out so it stays fresh. Even the best sunflower seed can't compare with a nice fat caterpillar or ripe dandelion seeds. Check stored seed in cans or bags weekly for signs of bug problems. Throw out infested seed in the trash to prevent perpetuating problems.

Now's a good opportunity to scrub the feeders with a weak bleach solution (1 part bleach to 10 parts water) and let them dry in the purifying sun. Also clean hummingbird feeders thoroughly each time you refill.

Your birdbath or garden pool may draw more birds than the feeders. Keep it brimming full with fresh water. Clean the birdbath frequently with a plastic dish scrubber. Don't use harsh cleansers—just put a handful of sand in the bottom of the bath to provide a natural abrasive when you scrub.

IN THE GARDEN

Summer is a great time for bird watching. Find a shady spot where you can sit and enjoy the abundant birdlife in your garden.

■ To locate nests, listen for the rhythmic peeps of baby birds as you stroll the garden or sit quietly on a bench, and watch for the parents carrying food.

■ Take inventory of nesting birds in your backyard, and write down nests, locations, and dates in a notebook so that you can compare it from year to year.

■ Continue putting out nesting materials. Some birds, including doves, robins, and chipping sparrows, nest more than once a year. They may reuse the first nest or build a new one.

■ Watch for birds like tanagers, grosbeaks, and orioles that usually stay in the treetops to come down to garden level for caterpillars and other insects.

■ Don't be too quick to adopt an orphan baby bird. Many birds leave the nest before they can fly, hiding in shrubbery or garden undergrowth for a few days until their wings are ready.

■ In early summer, plant a hedge or windbreak of sunflowers or corn; birds will devour the tasty seeds for weeks.

Change of Seasons

IN midsummer, when late nesters like goldfinches and cedar waxwings are still working on weaving their nests, other birds are already beginning to congregate in premigration flocks. Watch for swallows perching on utility wires in ever-growing groups, and flocks of grackles and other blackbirds crossing the sky before sunset.

Plumage changes take place as birds undergo "postnuptial" molt after the breeding season. It's fun to try to identify feathers that you find in your yard. Enjoy a last concert of morning bird song. As birds' hormonal levels change after nesting, they sing less and less. By late summer, very few birds are still singing, especially in the heat of the day.

Fall Almanac

FALL brings big changes in the cast of characters you'll see at your bird feeders and in your yard. Songbirds began migrating south as early as August; by early October, winter birds have settled in, while your summer birds are long gone. In the meantime, though, there are plenty of surprises in the garden as migrating birds stop over for a rest or for refueling.

Watch for changes in plumage among your backyard birds in the fall. Male goldfinches, grosbeaks, tanagers, orioles, and others lose their brilliant colors and switch to winter drab, mostly olive green. Starlings show a scattering of light-colored "stars" at the tips of their feathers.

Autumn marks the switch for birds from insects to seeds. Many male birds also change from bright breeding plumage to duller colors as fall arrives.

AT THE FEEDER

Your feeding station will receive heavy traffic as cold weather sets in, so fall is the time to clean and stock feeders and to stock up on birdseed. Repair any loose perches, weak corners, and other structural points; rickety feeders that may have held up to light summer traffic need to be in tip-top shape for the busy season. A single woodpecker can monopolize a suet feeder for most of the day. So put out several suet feeders to give all your resident birds a turn, and replace old suet with fresh blocks or chunks. Stock a very low tray feeder (1 foot or less above the ground) with cracked corn for mourning doves, who gather in flocks to feed in the fall. Keep the hummingbird and other nectar feeders up as long as you dare, until freezing temperatures threaten; more than one late migrant has been saved by a forgotten feeder. Also keep your birdbath brimming, as fresh water is vital for birds year-round. Remove fallen leaves from birdbaths daily.

FALL FEEDING
at a glance

Your fall to-dos should include:

■ Invest in new feeders—you can never have too many! Try buying a suet feeder, nut feeder, or another specialty type of feeder that you don't already have.

■ Clean out birdseed storage bins and inspect remaining stored seed. If you find seed that's infested with insects, discard it on the compost pile.

■ Freshen the mulch beneath your feeders. Spread a 2-inch-thick layer of wood chips or bark mulch over the area where seeds and hulls usually fall.

■ Collect ripe berries of hollies (*Ilex* spp.), sumacs (*Rhus* spp.), and other shrubs, as well as weed seeds, flower seeds, and nuts for the feeders.

■ Set up a salt block to attract finches, siskins, and other birds.

IN THE GARDEN

Fall is perfect planting and transplanting time for trees and shrubs. The soil stays warmer than the air for weeks or months, giving roots time to establish. Planting container shrubs and trees is simple: Dig a hole that's as deep as the pot is wide. Pull the shrub out of the container, set it in the hole, backfill with soil, and water deeply. Shrubs with berries on them, like holly, may attract birds the same day you plant them.

There are plenty of ways to provide bird treats in your garden in fall. Try some of these ideas:

■ Keep an eye on any berries or fruits in your yard. They're prime foods for birds that may alight during migration.

■ Listen for the quiet twitters and sharp *chip!* notes that betray the presence of song sparrows, white-throats, and other hard-to-see native sparrows around your yard. In the fall, a bounty of ripening seeds on garden plants, grasses, and weeds brings flocks of these little brown birds to backyards. They may stop at abundant seed patches for a morning or a whole week, but they're small, quick-moving, and wary of people, so you'll hear them more often than you'll see them.

■ Check garden centers and nurseries for viburnums, bayberries, and other shrubs that are already full of berries. Cart them home carefully so as not to dislodge the fruit, pop them into the garden, and the birds will reap the benefits immediately.

■ Look for end-of-the-season sales at nurseries and garden centers. Trees and shrubs—usually the biggest investment you'll make when creating a bird-friendly yard—are often available at half-price then.

Migration Notes

IN the fall, birds like warblers, swifts, flycatchers, and swallows that eat mostly insects are the first to depart from colder areas. They head for warm-winter regions where their food supply will keep on flying, creeping, or crawling all winter long.

It's much easier to keep track of new birds arriving than to notice the departures among backyard birds. For example, by the time it dawns on you that you haven't seen a chipping sparrow lately, the birds may have been gone for a week or more. To keep track, jot down on your wall calendar a twice-a-week census of who's around, both at feeders and in the yard. Be sure to note how many birds of each species you see. Looking back over your fall calendar, you can see at a glance when populations swell during migration or with the arrival of winter residents. Next fall, hang last year's calendar next to the current one and you'll have a good idea when to expect the first junco or when to wave goodbye to the orioles.

Your local forecast also contains clues that can help you figure out when migrating birds will arrive. Birds like to fly ahead of cold fronts because they can take advantage of the tailwind to make their journey faster and easier. When the weather report says "cold front coming in," chances are your yard will be teeming with birds the next day.

HARVESTING SEED

Late summer into early fall is prime time for seedheads to mature in the garden. Beating the birds to the best seeds can be a challenge because they're monitoring the ripeness of the seedheads even more often than you are. Thus, the presence of seed eaters such as goldfinches at your sunflowers, zinnias, or other seed-bearing plants is a sign for you to start collecting if you intend to put aside any ripe seeds for later feeder use.

Harvesting seeds before they are completely ripe helps you beat the birds. Many seeds continue to ripen even if harvested from the plant when green. In general, look for seedheads that have filled out with plump green seeds that are beginning to turn yellow. These seeds usually will dry to a ripe golden or brown color even if removed from the plant.

If you intend to use seedheads in wreaths, swags, or bundles, allow long stems when picking. Otherwise, you can snip individual clusters into a large brown paper sack. To separate the seeds, tightly close the sack and shake briskly, causing the ripe seeds to fall free from the seedhead. Pour off the seeds into containers for later use.

If you're picking seeds that aren't fully ripe, spread the seedheads in shallow cardboard trays in a dry place protected from birds and rodents. Check the seeds daily, and when they're ripe, transfer the seedheads to paper bags to shake off the seeds as described above.

Many flowers and weeds lend themselves to seed collecting. It's fun to observe which birds prefer which seeds when you offer them later at the feeder. Here are some easy ones to get you started:

- Amaranths
- Annual sunflower
- Chicory
- Purple coneflower (*Echinacea purpurea*)
- Cosmos (*Cosmos sulphureus, C. bipinnatus*)
- Garden balsam (*Impatiens balsamina*)
- Lamb's-quarters
- Lettuce
- Marigolds
- Safflower (*Carthamus tinctorius*)
- Zinnias

Winter Almanac

THE main reason that feeder traffic takes a dramatic jump in winter is that natural food is much scarcer then. The few foods that do remain are hard to find, and birds can save considerable precious energy by zeroing in on your feeder instead of hunting for their own breakfast, lunch, and dinner. In cold-winter areas, insects are just a summer memory, except for the stray cocoon or overwintering egg. Fruits and seeds are mostly eaten, too, by the time winter rolls around.

COMINGS AND GOINGS

Not only is the demand higher for bird-feeder foods in winter, but the sheer number of birds that visit your yard increases because of flocking patterns. Blackbirds and house finches may arrive in large flocks; cardinals, finches, grosbeaks, sparrows, and other birds now pal around in groups instead of living the solitary life.

The cast of characters at your feeder remains fairly stable in winter, except that the numbers will swell temporarily when bad weather moves in. Occasional rare birds, either unusual for your region or unusual for your feeder, also appear at feeders in the winter, driven by hunger.

If you live in the Deep South or southern California, the scene at your winter feeders may be quite different than the view in cold, snowy areas. Rufous and black-chinned hummungbirds are in winter residence along the Gulf coast, busily visiting nectar feeders. Red-breasted nuthatches, a southern rarity in spring and summer except during migration, now settle in across the southern half of the country for a sunny winter vacation, as do chipping sparrows and fox sparrows. In the West, the beautiful varied thrush moves in, giving winter feeder keepers all the way to Baja some color to enjoy. Western and mountain bluebirds move into the southern regions of the West. In the Deep South and along the southern Atlantic coast, house wrens may visit for mealworms; catbirds, robins, and brown thrashers may turn up at the chopped suet or fruit feeder; and Bullock's and Baltimore orioles may grace the nectar feeder. As the days gradually start to lengthen at the end of winter, you'll notice that the birds at your feeders are beginning to behave differently. Male cardinals, juncos, native sparrows, and other males of the same species that formerly ate companionably side by side now become short-tempered, turning to each other with flashing wings and threatening opened beaks. It's only natural—longer daylight hours kick the reproductive hormones into gear, and battles over elbow-room and mates become a more frequent occurrence. Doves, owls, and woodpeckers are among the earliest to actually start a family, often in late winter.

At the Feeder

Bird feeders are at their busiest in winter. And the most important rule of winter feeding is: Be prepared. Storms can move in quickly, making that little jaunt to the birdseed store a nightmare or just plain impossible.

Is a big snow coming? Just take a look at the feeders. If they are jam-packed with birds and they linger until past their usual last-call time, you can bet bad weather is on the way.

You'll appreciate your freezer and pantry in the winter months, too, if you have stockpiled them with bird treats such as chopped suet, raw hamburger, meat scraps, leftovers, and nuts. Grain-based foods from the kitchen, such as cereal recipes, bread crumbs, and baked goods, are a hit with many kinds of birds. Frozen or dried fruits and berries come in handy for bluebirds, catbirds, robins, thrashers, wrens, and other birds that usually eschew seeds. (Put out cracked corn, ear corn, and apple peelings for squirrels, deer, and other wildlife, as well.)

If you've included a salt block at your feeding area, you'll see it's as popular in winter as at other times of the year. Winter brings winter finches sweeping down irregularly

WINTER FEEDING
at a glance

Help your feathered friends get through winter without a struggle.

■ Keep feeders free of ice and snow. Erect lean-tos or add roofs so that at least some feeders are covered.

■ Save leftover soft foods, such as bread and pancakes, for catbirds, robins, wrens, and other soft-food eaters. If you run out of kitchen leftovers, serve these birds moistened dog food.

■ Recycle your Christmas tree into a windbreak alongside a low-level tray feeder.

■ Make homemade treats for the birds, such as the ever-popular peanut butter–smeared pinecones.

from the North, and salt is a big hit with these unusual birds.

Birds still search for water in winter, too. Since most natural sources of water are frozen, a bird-bath or other water feature free of ice will make your yard a magnet for birds. They splash about in fresh water even when the temperature is frigid, as long as they find a sunny perch afterward where they can dry their feathers. Run an immersible heater to the birdbath, or try a solar birdbath that uses the sun's heat to keep water from freezing. At the very least, you can put out a shallow pan or clay saucer of warm water once a day. Take it into the house when the water begins to freeze.

IN THE GARDEN

Any berries or fruits left in your garden won't last long in winter. No matter how unappealing those few shriveled apples clinging to the tree may look to you, to birds they're a real find. Keep your eyes on your garden in winter and you may be in store for a show.

■ Sparrows, juncos, titmice, and chickadees will work the last tiny

(continued on page 170)

Winter Food Plants

STOCKING YOUR yard with plants that hold their seeds, berries, or cones into the winter months is a great way to draw foraging thrushes, cedar waxwings, and other birds that may be reluctant to visit a feeding station. Natural foods also provide a welcome change of pace for your feeder regulars. All conifers are a good source of winter food, but consider rounding out the menu with a few other possibilities, such as the following:

Long-Lasting Seedheads

Amaranths (*Amaranthus* spp.): Annual weeds or decorative garden plants, this genus holds seed-packed fuzzy spikes relished throughout the cold months by buntings, doves, finches, goldfinches, juncos, horned larks, pheasants, quail, redpolls, native sparrows, and towhees.

Ragweeds (*Ambrosia* spp.): Common annual weeds, ranging from knee-high to head height, depending on species, produce abundant small, oily seeds sought by cardinals, doves, finches, and many other birds.

Big bluestem (*Andropogon gerardii*): Very tall native perennial prairie grass, to 6 feet, with interesting "turkey foot"–shaped seedheads that eventually keel over in late winter, providing food for juncos, native sparrows, towhees, and other ground-feeding birds.

Broomsedge (*A. virginicus*): Perennial grass almost identical to little bluestem (*Schizachyrium scoparium*), with more of a "whisk-broom" look near the tops of the stems; acquires rich orangeish color in fall and winter. Small seeds sought by rosy finches, juncos, native sparrows, and game birds.

Little bluestem (*Schizachyrium scoparium*): Clump-forming native perennial prairie grass that grows to 3 feet tall and turns beautiful warm orange in fall and winter. Fuzzy seed clusters along stems furnish food for finches, game birds, juncos, and native sparrows, as well as small mammals.

Winter Berries or Fruit

Manzanitas (*Arctostaphlyos* spp.): Striking smooth, red bark characterizes many of the shrubby species of this western and southwestern genus, which also includes ground-hugging bearberry (*A. uva-ursi*). Red or brown berries are prime food for grouse, grosbeaks, jays, mockingbirds, and fox sparrows as well as for small mammals—skunks particularly like them!

Hackberries (*Celtis laevigata, C. occidentalis,* and other spp.): Lovely shade trees with interesting warty gray bark and a multitude of small fruits that ripen in late fall to early winter. Source of food for catbirds, flickers, jays, mockingbirds, orioles, robins, sapsuckers, starlings, thrashers, thrushes, titmice, woodpeckers, and wrens, which devour the bounty while still on the tree. Towhees, fox sparrows, and other native sparrows join in the feast when the fruit drops.

Persimmons (*Diospyros virginiana, D. texana*): Native trees with alligator-hide–checkered bark; large, simple leaves; and astringent orange to orange-red fleshy fruit that softens and sweetens when ripe. Beloved by bluebirds, catbirds, mockingbirds, robins, sapsuckers, starlings, wild turkeys, yellow-rumped warblers, and waxwings. Also a favorite of the raccoon and its close relative, the unusual ring-tailed cat of Texas, the Southwest, and West.

Cedars (*Juniperus* spp.): Deep green or gray-green conifers with often prickly foliage and lovely blue berries, much sought by bluebirds, catbirds, crossbills, doves, finches, flickers, grosbeaks, jays, mockingbirds, robins, sapsuckers, thrashers, thrushes, yellow-rumped warblers, and waxwings, as well as game birds.

Sumacs (*Rhus* spp.): Native shrubs or small trees with foliage that turns brilliant red to orange in fall and dense, pointed clusters of red (white in some species) fuzzy berries held upright. A food of last resort, the berries are eaten in winter by crows, ruffed grouse, pigeons, quail, wild turkeys, and many songbirds, including bluebirds, cardinals, catbirds, purple finches, flickers, jays, magpies, mockingbirds, starlings, thrushes, woodpeckers, and wrens.

Greenbriers (*Smilax* spp.): Evergreen or deciduous native climbers, some thorny-stemmed, absent in parts of the West and abundant in the Southeast. Berries may be yellow, black, blue, or green and are devoured eagerly by many birds: Bluebirds, catbirds, fish crows, flickers, mockingbirds, robins, fox sparrows, white-throated sparrows, thrushes, cedar waxwings, and pileated woodpeckers are among the prime customers.

seeds from flower and weed seed-heads, leaving behind a bare stalk or wisps of fiber.

■ Tree seeds attract the attention of hungry seed eaters now. Look for grosbeaks, cardinals, and finches in your ash trees, tulip poplars, alders, box elders, locusts, and any other trees with seeds still attached. Seeds of catalpa trees are a big favorite with evening grosbeaks, who hang upside down like parrots to extract the seeds from the beanlike pods.

■ Keep an eye on your shrub roses or wild roses at the edge of your yard, as rose hips are a favorite winter food for birds.

You can serve seed directly on the ground in winter—just make sure you clear away any loose snow before scattering the seed.

SNOW AND ICE STORMS

When winter storms hit your area, it's hard times for birds. Because the ground is covered with snow or ice, birds have to scratch vigorously to reach seeds that may—or may not—be underneath the white stuff. Tree buds, berries, nuts, and even the last withered crabapples may be encased in ice or frozen to impenetrable hardness. Weed stems are bent and bowed under a layer of snow.

It's during times like these that birds turn to the feeder for sustenance. Although you can't serve hot cocoa to your birds, you can do the next best thing: Give them high-fat, high-carbohydrate foods that will quickly refuel their calorie-burning bodies and supply the store of energy they need to survive through long, cold nights. Add bacon grease, doughnuts, nuts, and peanut-butter recipes to the menu of standard seeds and suet.

Birds are out early the morning after a storm, and you should be, too. Keeping your guests waiting is not just rude, it's dangerous to their well-being.

At least make sure the covered feeders are fully stocked before you turn in for the night. You mission is to keep food available as long as birds need it. Falling snow or freezing rain and ice can cover feeders fast, so erect lean-tos and other temporary shelters over and around your feeders to divert falling or drifting snow.

Lots of items will do the trick as a temporary lean-to. Any piece of stiff, flat material will work. Use two or three sturdy sticks or 2 × 4s to prop up the protective shelter. Make sure the supports are strong and evenly spaced so that the weight of snow doesn't cause a collapse of your impromptu shelter.

If you have a multitude of customers, you can serve seed directly on the ground. (You can also put out bread and other baked goods on the ground so the small birds and robins can get their share without fighting the competition at the feeder.) Clear the loose snow, scatter the food, and before you get back in the house, the birds will be eating. If snow keeps falling, sweep aside the new snow as often as you have time and patience to do so.

HOLIDAY TREATS

High-fat, high-caloric bird treats and a smorgasbord of other delights help birds conserve precious energy in winter. They can fill their bellies on your homemade gifts without expending calories searching the woods and fields for sustenance.

Nuts fill the bill for bird treats perfectly. Look at making holiday bird treats as the perfect reason for cleaning your kitchen cupboards. Start by ransacking the pantry shelves—perhaps you'll find a half-empty box of raisins petrified to break-your-tooth dryness. If so, dump them into a bowl along with the nuts, then add the last couple of inches from an old bottle of molasses and the remains of a couple of boxes of cornmeal. To give the treats a little more substance, add a few handfuls of fine-chopped suet—then mix everything together. Once the ingredients are thoroughly mixed, mold the mixture into small balls. Wrap each ball a few times around with light-gauge wire for hanging, then store the balls in the freezer until you need them. These suet balls are perfect for decorating young hemlocks or bare-branched shrubs.

Decorations for Birds

YOU can decorate your yard with plenty of wonderful bird-pleasing fare—without breaking the bank.

■ Include some branches of berries when you fill your window boxes with fresh greenery for Christmas. Birds will soon find branches of holly, both the traditional evergreen type and the interesting deciduous varieties. Birds also like bayberries or juniper berries. The berries may attract robins, mocking-birds, waxwings, yellow-rumped warblers, and other berry lovers.

■ Hang a wreath (or two or three) for the birds. A giant sunflower head makes a great instant wreath. Remove the center and add a decorative touch with a cluster of millet spray or peanuts wired together. You may be able to find sunflower heads at craft shops or bird supply stores. Plan ahead for next year: Make a note on the August page of your calendar to set aside some of your own garden sunflower heads for making Christmas bird wreaths.

■ Prepare for a bird Christmas by planting a spruce, fir, hemlock, pine, or other evergreen in fall so it's ready for embellishment at holiday time.

■ Ask your grocer for old grapes that are past their prime. You can often collect pounds of grapes (or other old fruit, for that matter) for free or only a dollar or two. Hang or wire the bunches of grapes to trees and shrubs around your yard and you may attract mockingbirds, robins, cedar waxwings, and bluebirds.

■ Slice oranges into ¼-inch rounds and hang on tree limbs from strings sewn through the rind.

■ Make mini-wreaths of raisins by threading them onto a circle of wire.

■ Make peanut butter–stuffed pinecones. Using a spoon, spread extra-chunky peanut butter onto the cone, then loop a piece of wire or string beneath the first row of scales for hanging. You can stretch that expensive peanut butter by mixing it with ground suet or cornmeal, but don't roll the cone in birdseed. Not all peanut-butter eaters eat birdseed mix.

Feeding through the Seasons

Q During migration—spring and fall—I often see new and different birds at my feeders. Should I keep putting out the same food that my regular birds—chickadees, jays, and cardinals—eat? Or do these welcome visitors need something different to eat?

A You should tailor your menu to the needs of the migrants you expect to see, or add new foods quickly once they arrive. Fruit, suet, peanut butter, bread crumbs, and mealworms are popular with orioles, tanagers, thrushes, and other travelers that eat mostly insects. These delicacies may entice them to linger a little longer at your feeding station. They will also come to drink and bathe in fresh water, especially if you add a drip device so the birds can hear the water from a distance.

Q At various times throughout the year I seem to be plagued by a rodent problem at my feeders. What can I do to get rid of these undesirable guests?

A Among the many furry rodents that visit your bird-feeding stations, mice and rats may show up for their share of the handouts, particularly if you allow seed and other food to lie on the ground.

Traps are the quickest and most reliable way to eliminate a rodent problem. Don't use the old-fashioned traps that whack, though, because they can also snag a bird or flying squirrel. Use only live traps that allow animals to enter but not leave, and take the rodents to a wild area far from your home to release them. (Make sure you wear heavy leather gloves to protect yourself from bites and disease.)

To prevent rodent problems before they start, practice good sanitation around the feeder area. Avoid feeding birds on the ground, and shovel up spilled seed regularly.

Weeds for All Seasons

THE fact is, birds love weeds. To birds, weeds mean just one thing: food, and lots of it. Find a stand of giant ragweed in winter, and you're sure to find a horde of cardinals, finches, and native sparrows, which come to feast on the abundant seeds until the spiky seedheads are picked clean. Same thing with lamb's-quarters: A thicket of the 4-foot-tall plants will attract scores of buntings, chickadees, finches, siskins, sparrows, and others. In spring and summer, weed leaves hide many a tasty insect tidbit, and when weed seeds ripen, the bounty draws birds from far and wide. Look for goldfinches in thistle patches, and indigo buntings, white-crowned sparrows, and other native sparrows wherever dandelions raise their fluffy seedheads.

Why do birds love the plants we scorn? Well, most weed seeds are rich in oil and calories, an important consideration when you're a creature whose daily life consists of finding enough food to keep your rapid-fire metabolism on track. Plus, weeds are familiar plants. Birds know just where their fa-vorite weeds are likely to spring up year after year. They know when seeds will ripen, and they know just the right technique for foraging for the seeds. And weeds tend to grow in dense stands, so little time or energy is wasted—it's an all-you-can-eat avian meal in a single sitting.

BEST OF THE BUNCH

The number-one weed for birds is the pretty annual grass known as foxtail, or bristlegrass. You've probably seen the fuzzy spikes of this common weed along roadsides and fields nearby, or even sprouting in your own flowerbeds. The bristly seedheads may be arching or they may stand erect, depending on species, but birds gobble them no matter what position they're in. Practically every seed-eating bird in America seeks out foxtail grass, a close cousin of the millet so popular at the feeder. Doves, ducks, grouse, quail, and other game birds are huge fans. Among the songbird clan, everyone from cardinals and grosbeaks to sparrows and

FOUR SEASONS OF WEEDS FOR BIRDS

FAMILIAR weeds that we remove from our gardens are great sources of food for many birds. So accept a bit of untidiness during the growing season and leave some weeds standing for the fall and winter.

WEED	DESCRIPTION	COMMENTS
Pigweeds (*Amaranthus* spp.)	30-plus species of coarse, annual weeds with fuzzy stalks of tiny flowers and seeds	Eagerly eaten by all small seed-eating birds, including buntings, doves, finches, goldfinches, juncos, horned larks, pheasant, quail, redpolls, native sparrows, and towhees. Large-beaked rose-breasted grosbeaks also devour the seeds.
Ragweeds (*Ambrosia* spp.)	Annual and exceedingly common weeds whose spikes of tiny, non-descript flowers produce masses of airborne irritating pollen, the bane of the allergy-prone	Seeds relished by song sparrows, swamp sparrows, white-throated sparrows, and other native sparrows; also black-birds, bobolinks, buntings, crossbills, grosbeaks, juncos, horned larks, meadowlarks, redpolls, robins, siskins, towhees, and even cedar waxwings.
Star-thistles (napa star-thistle, *Centaurea melitensis*; yellow star-thistle, *C. solstitialis*)	Common annual prickly plants of western grainfields, especially in California; flowers mature to bristly clusters of seeds	Seeds sought by mourning doves, house finches, goldfinches, Oregon juncos, California quail, pine siskins, golden-crowned and other western native sparrows, titmice, and towhees.
Lamb's-quarters (*Chenopodium album*)	Annual weed growing to 4 feet tall; multiple branches from single stem; arrow-shaped leaves and packed clusters of small, greenish flowers	Oily seeds eagerly sought by doves, grouse, quail, and other game birds as well as buntings, finches, goldfinches, juncos, horned larks, pyrrhuloxia, redpolls, and native sparrows.
Chicory (*Cichorium intybus*)	Tall perennial weed with dandelion-like rosette of toothed leaves in winter, followed by a tall, branching stem of light blue flowers in spring and summer	Buntings, finches, juncos, siskins, and native sparrows eat the seeds.
Filarees (*Erodium* spp.)	Also known as stork's bill, these annual weeds are especially common in the West; fernlike leaves and dainty pink-purple flowers mature into long, pointy seeds	Highly popular with almost all small seed-eating birds, including blackbirds, buntings, doves, finches, goldfinches, juncos, horned larks, meadowlarks, quail, siskins, native sparrows, varied thrush, towhees, wrens, and waxwings.
Smartweeds (*Polygonum* spp.)	Ultracommon annual weeds, sprawling in habit, low to tall in height, with tight-packed spikes of tiny, usually pink or white flowers	Highly popular with doves, grouse, quail, and other game birds, and almost all seed-eating songbirds such as black-birds, buntings, finches, goldfinches, juncos, horned larks, redpolls, and nearly all native sparrows.
Chickweed (*Stellaria media*)	Winter annual weed that sprouts in fall on bare ground; grows in a low, sprawling clump of tiny green leaves and even smaller white flowers that bloom in winter to early spring	White-crowned, white-throated, and other native sparrows relish the multitude of tiny seeds, which ripen during spring sparrow migration. Also sought by buntings, doves, finches, gold-finches, juncos, horned larks, quail, pine siskins, and towhees.
Dandelion (*Taraxacum officinale*)	Familiar perennial weed with rosette of long, toothed leaves and familiar yellow flowers	Indigo buntings, goldfinches, pine siskins, and native sparrows adore the seeds. Look for groups of these birds and an occasional rose-breasted grosbeak at dandelion patches during spring migration. Yellow-headed blackbirds, Brewer's blackbirds, and towhees also enjoy the seeds.

KEY
Seasons when seeds are plentiful: ■Spring ■Summer ■Fall ■Winter

thrashers—at least 46 species—relish the small, crunchy seeds. This is one of the most abundant American weeds—and one of the easiest to collect for later offerings at the feeder.

INVITING WEEDS INTO THE GARDEN

It goes against the grain for most gardeners, but adding weeds to the backyard bird garden is an excellent way to bring in the birds. That doesn't mean you need to rush out and plant weeds—they'll pop up just fine on their own. It does mean that you'll need to shift your perspective a bit. Think of that thicket of lamb's-quarters and dock as sparrow food and junco food.

If you can tolerate a few weeds in your yard—or better yet, if you have a discreet corner that you can let "go wild" with weeds—you'll increase your bird life by a bushel. Plus you'll get to observe the interesting ways birds devour different seeds. You may see an indigo bunting neatly pulling one tuft after another from a dandelion puff, or perhaps a tree sparrow hopping off the ground to pull down a seedhead of curly dock so it can stand on the stem while it eats.

Of course, in areas like your vegetable garden, you'll want to keep weeds under control. The magic word for weed control is mulch. A layer of grass clippings or shredded bark will keep weeds at bay. Organic mulches gradually decompose, so renew yours with a fresh layer as often as needed. Put down a layer of mulch as soon as you set out new plants, and you'll stop the weeds in their tracks. If you sow seeds in the garden, you'll still need to hand-weed until your seedlings are big enough to mulch around.

Seeds from perennial weed chicory are popular with finches.

Make weeding easy with an arsenal of the right tools. A long-bladed dandelion fork is great for getting out deep-rooted chicory. A long-handled hoe can't be beat for slicing off seedling weeds. A hand-held hoe is handy for weeding in tight quarters or beneath shrubs. To get out tough weeds, including tree seedlings, grasp the weed firmly at the soil surface with a pair of pliers and twist as you pull.

Insects for All Seasons

PRACTICALLY every bird eats insects—and if it weren't for birds keeping insects in check, insect populations would skyrocket in no time. Some birds eat more insects than other birds. The purple martin, which loops through the air, bill agape, scoops up thousands of flying insects every day, from dragonflies to mosquitoes.

Even birds that depend mostly on seeds, such as native sparrows, also consume huge quantities of insects. You may even begin to appreciate starlings when you realize that they enthusiastically devour ants,

Preferred Bugs

AS with feeder foods, birds also have their preferences when it comes to insects. It's fascinating to try to figure out who's eating what in your backyard. You can learn a lot just by watching birds at work. If a bird lingers at a plant and is obviously picking off insects, go find out what it's eating. You may discover that the bark is teeming with ants, or that tiny green caterpillars are looping their way through the leaves.

Don't bother trying to figure out what birds to attract to get rid of specific insects, though. While you will surely appreciate the efforts of grosbeaks in eating potato bugs, all bird efforts are vital in the grand scheme of things. Natural life is a balance, and birds help keep it that way.

Quick Reference	BUGS THE BIRDS LOVE

BIRDS eat insects found in their native habitat. Here are a few of the top bug menu items of some common birds.

BIRDS	FAVORED INSECT FOODS*
Red-winged blackbird	Beetles, caddis flies, cankerworms, gypsy moths and tent caterpillars, grasshoppers, grubs, mayflies, moths, spiders
Yellow-headed blackbird	Alfalfa weevils, beetles, caterpillars, grasshoppers
Eastern bluebird	Beetles, crickets, grasshoppers, katydids
Mountain bluebird	Beetles, weevils
Western bluebird	Beetles, crickets, grasshoppers
Indigo bunting	Aphids, beetles, cankerworms, cicadas, grasshoppers
Painted bunting	Cankerworms, caterpillars, crickets, flies, grasshoppers, spiders, wasps, boll weevils
Cardinal	Aphids, beetles, caterpillars, cicadas, crickets, codling moths, scale insects, spiders, termites
Black-capped chickadee	Caterpillars, codling moths, codling moth caterpillars
Flickers, all races	Ants
Common grackle	Ants, beetles—Japanese, June, and others—cicadas, earthworms, flies, grubs, grasshoppers, boll weevils
Black-headed grosbeak	Bees, beetles, cankerworms, codling moth caterpillars, flies, grasshoppers, scale insects, spiders, wasps
Evening grosbeak	Beetles, spruce budworm, cankerworms
Rose-breasted grosbeak	Colorado potato beetle and other beetles, cankerworms, tent caterpillars, gypsy moth caterpillars, grasshoppers

millipedes, spiders, and wasps—and countless Japanese beetle grubs.

Because of their appetite for insects and arachnids, such as spiders and ticks, attracting birds to your yard means better health for your trees and plants. Birds work tirelessly all year to glean insect eggs, young, adults, and cocoons from their hiding places among foliage, in bark crevices, or under leaf litter on the ground. Watch any bird as it moves about your yard, and its insect-searching behavior will be evident.

SUMMER SELECTIONS

In summer, many birds use insects as a main staple of their diet. Everywhere you look you'll find

Quick Reference	BUGS THE BIRDS LOVE—CONTINUED
BIRDS	**FAVORED INSECT FOODS***
Blue jay	May beetles and other beetles, tent caterpillars, gypsy moth caterpillars, grasshoppers, spiders
Junco	Ants, beetles, caterpillars, spiders, wasps, weevils
Black-billed magpie	Flies, grasshoppers, maggots, ticks
Yellow-billed magpie	Ants, bees, beetles, grasshoppers, wasps
Northern oriole	Caterpillars, especially hairy ones such as gypsy moths
Orchard oriole	Ants, aphids, beetles, cankerworms, caterpillars, crickets, grasshoppers, mayflies
Robin	Earthworms; also beetles, cicadas, grasshoppers, termites
Chipping sparrow	Ants, leaf beetles, caterpillars, grasshoppers, leafhoppers
Song sparrow	Ants, army worms, beetles, cutworms, grasshoppers, ichneumon flies, wasps, many others
White-crowned sparrow	Beetles, caterpillars, flies, mosquitoes, spiders
White-throated sparrow	Ants, beetles, flies
Plain titmouse	Aphids, true bugs, leafhoppers, scale insects, many others
Tufted titmouse	Mainly caterpillars
Downy woodpecker	Carpenter ants, click beetles, spruce beetles, wood borers, cicadas, moths, nut weevils, pine weevils, many others
Hairy woodpecker	Mostly larvae of wood borers
Pileated woodpecker	Carpenter ants, wood-boring beetles

*Includes earthworms and arachnids, such as spiders, which are not insects.

caterpillars and other delectable tidbits, and birds take advantage of such easy pickings. Later, when seeds ripen and insects become scarce, finches and other seed eaters return to a seed-based diet.

Early to midsummer, when nesting is at its peak, many insects are reaching their highest populations. That dovetails nicely from a bird's-eye perspective because there is abundant protein-packed food available just when nestlings need it most. Nestling birds aren't capable of cracking seeds or eating tough-skinned fruits with their tender bills, so parents seek bite-sized bugs to stuff in their hungry mouths. By the time young birds have left the nest and are learning to hunt on their own, insects fill every nook and cranny of the yard and wild places.

TRAVEL PLANS

Migrant songbirds that retreat from cold areas for the winter months are often birds that depend mainly on insects. Swallows, martins, and swifts, which catch insects on the wing, are among the earliest to move southward. They can't take any chances of a sudden cold front moving in and wiping out their sole food supply.

Unfortunately, spring weather is full of surprises, and purple martins are sometimes caught by a late-season cold snap after they have already started nesting in your backyard. Your local bait shop, however, can be the key to their survival: $5 worth of mealworms, offered in an open tray feeder, fills a lot of martin bellies.

Most flycatchers, orioles, tanagers, vireos, and warblers migrate early, too, long before frost creeps in to still the insect life. These birds can supplement their diet with berries, fruit, and sometimes seeds, so a few hardy souls may linger into winter. These stragglers are one reason why soft food can be so valuable at your feeding station when Old Man Winter arrives. When a sudden snowstorm sur-prises a lingering catbird or flock of robins and they can't find their usual fare, they'll welcome a handout from you. Ground suet, bread, special recipes, or other soft foods can mean the difference between life and death for these birds.

Seed-eating birds such as finches and juncos make less dramatic long-distance flights in fall because their natural food is available in nearby climates that may be only a few hundred miles south. Crows, jays, and woodpeckers may not move on at all, being able to find food in any weather. (And that means you'll get to enjoy watching them all winter long.)

AVIAN PEST CONTROL

Birds are our best allies in restoring the balance of insects in yard and garden. In turn, pesticides disrupt the natural equilibrium of your yard. Although your goal is to get rid of a particular pest when you reach for a bottle of pesticide, you are probably also killing off populations of other insects. Loss of these insects makes it harder for your backyard birds to find the insects they need. Chemicals may also have adverse effects on birds directly; DDT, for example, was rightfully notorious for causing thin eggshells that wouldn't support the weight of parent birds, as well as other dangers. Chemicals such as diazinon—only a few years ago a common ingredient of "green lawn" treatments on garden store shelves, but which has since been banned—may also have serious repercussions for bird health, as well as for human and pet health.

Keep your yard free of pesticides, and let the bird crew do the work of keeping insects in balance. After all, they've had a few million years of practice.

Mosquitoes and Moths

TO birds, the whine of a mosquito sounds like the dinner bell. Buntings, martins, native sparrows, swallows, and swifts include these prolific, widespread, and generally slow-moving insects in their diets. However, you certainly don't want to breed mosquitoes to attract birds. Exercise common sense in mosquito control by emptying stray water-filled containers (such as forgotten buckets) that may serve as breeding sites. Don't overlook the rain gutters, as clogged gutters can support large numbers of larvae. The birds in your yard will do their best to keep up with the natural mosquito population.

Moths—as well as their eggs, caterpillars, and cocoons—make superb bird food. Bluebirds, flycatchers, orioles, phoebes, robins, and dozens of other species make moths a staple in their diets. In winter, the tough, fibrous cocoons of many moth species are targets for chickadees and titmice, which work industriously to tear open the tough silk and get at the meaty morsel within. Eggs and egg masses of moths are a big hit with nuthatches, woodpeckers, and other guardians of the trees. Moths on the wing make a quick snack for any bird near enough to grab a bite. Even screech owls seek out moths, particularly the large, fat-bodied silkworm moths, such as the cecropia.

Best Backyard Plants for Birds

While birdfeeders and bird baths certainly put out the welcome mat for our avian friends, you can make your landscape even more bird-friendly with the addition of plants the birds love. This quick reference guide details the best annuals, perennials, berry and native plants, evergreens, grasses, and shrubs to grow to make your yard even more hospitable to these feathered creatures.

Quick Reference — FAVORITE ANNUALS FOR BIRDS

HERE are seven annuals that are favorites of a wide variety of birds. And the great thing about these plants is not only do birds love 'em, but they're easy to grow, too. Just sow the seeds directly in the ground—soon you'll have a garden for the birds.

PLANT NAMES	BIRDS ATTRACTED	PLANT DESCRIPTION	CULTURE	COMMENTS
Bachelor's-button (*Centaurea cyanus*)	Finches, buntings, sparrows	2' to 3' branching plants with 1½" fringed flowers in blue, pink, rose, purple, and white from spring to fall	Sow in fall or early spring in full sun in average soil.	Sow seeds or plant transplants every 4 weeks for season-long bloom. Self-sows after the first year.
Garden balsam (*Impatiens balsamina*)	Flowers attract hummingbirds; seeds attract grosbeaks, cardinals, sparrows	1' to 2' succulent plants with pretty ruffled 2" flowers in pink, purple-pink, or white in mid- to late summer	Sow in early spring in full sun to shade in average soil.	Self-sows, but flower color changes to soft magenta purple.
Cosmos (*Cosmos* spp.)	Finches, sparrows, juncos, buntings	Airy 2' to 4' branching plants with fine foliage and lovely 3" to 4" flowers in a range of pinks, reds, yellow, and orange	Sow in spring in full sun in average soil.	Try unusual cultivars like 'Seashell', with rolled petals, and look for interesting edgings of contrasting color on flowers of self-sown plants.
Love-lies-bleeding (*Amaranthus caudatus*)	Finches, sparrows	Bushy 3' to 4' plants, often with vivid magenta stems; velvety-soft tiny flowers on dangling tassels up to 1' long	Sow in full sun in midspring when soil is warm, in average to poor soil.	Leave plants in the garden into winter to feed sparrows and other small seed-eating birds.
Mexican sunflower (*Tithonia rotundifolia*)	Flowers attract hummingbirds; seeds attract finches, buntings, cardinals, jays, titmice, chickadees, nuthatches	4' to 8' branching plants with large leaves and velvety stems; brilliant orange-red daisylike flowers from midsummer to early fall	Sow in full sun in average soil. Leave plenty of space for plants to spread their branches.	Try planting an entire bed or a hedge of these fabulous flowers.
Tickseed sunflower (*Bidens aristosa*)	Finches, buntings, chickadees, titmice, sparrows	2' to 5' airy, branching plants with ferny foliage, covered in buttery yellow daisylike flowers in mid- to late summer	Sow in early spring in full sun in average soil. Thrives in wet soil, too.	Self-sows very generously. Mulch to control seedlings or hoe lightly to uproot them.
Zinnias (*Zinnia* spp.)	Finches, sparrows, buntings, chickadees, titmice	Bright or pastel, flat or mounded flowers on bushy, branching plants; flowers and plants vary widely in size, depending on species and cultivar	Sow in midspring in full sun in average soil.	Powdery mildew may mar the foliage; plant lower-growing annuals in front to hide the mildewed zinnia leaves.

FAVORITE PERENNIALS FOR BIRDS

WHILE birds may enjoy almost any dense perennial garden because it provides good shelter and nesting sites, they'll be more likely to visit gardens that include some of the perennials listed below. You can also learn about more great perennials for birds by reading about bee balm, columbines, coneflowers, coral bells, salvias, and sunflowers, beginning on page 113.

PLANT NAMES	BIRDS ATTRACTED	PLANT DESCRIPTION	CULTURE
Coreopsis (*Coreopsis lanceolata* and other perennial spp.)	Flowers attract butterflies, which attract spiders and other insects eaten by many birds. Sparrows and finches eat seeds.	Mounds of lance-shaped or feathery-looking leaves topped by daisy-shaped gold flowers; species and cultivars range from 1' to 3' tall.	Grow in full sun, in average-to-rich, well-drained soil. Drought-tolerant. Zones 3 to 10.
Goldenrods (*Solidago* spp.)	Seeds attract sparrows; chickadees and other birds forage for insects on flowers and stems.	Clumps of leafy stems topped by plumes of tiny golden flowers from midsummer to fall. 18" to 6' tall, depending on species.	Grow in full sun in average, well-drained soil. Zones 3 to 10.
Anise hyssop (*Agastache foeniculum*)	Flowers attract bees and hummingbirds; finches and sparrows eat seeds.	Scalloped, gray-green leaves topped by branching spikes of tiny blue-purple flowers; 2' to 3' tall; plant smells like licorice.	Grow in full sun, in average-to-poor, well-drained soil. Zones 5 to 9.
Yellow giant hyssop (*Agastache nepetoides*)	Flowers attract hummingbirds; finches, buntings, and sparrows eat seeds; in winter, downy woodpeckers, chickadees, titmice, and yellow-rumped warblers eat insects and larvae overwintering in stems.	Beautiful vertical plant with stout, erect stems topped with branched spikes of tiny, green-yellow flowers.	Grow in shade to part sun in soil rich in organic matter; also grows in clay. Zones 3 to 8.
Mulleins (*Verbascum thapsus* and other spp.)	Goldfinches and other small birds eat seeds; in winter, downy woodpeckers, chickadees, titmice, yellow-rumped warblers, bluebirds, and others eat insects and larvae overwintering in seedhead stalks.	Gray, fuzzy leaves grow in a ground-hugging clump, from which rises a 3'- to 6'-tall spire covered in tiny, yellow or white blossoms.	Grow in full sun in average-to-poor, well-drained soil. Zones 3 to 8.
Garden phlox (*Phlox paniculata*, *P. maculata*)	Flowers attract butterflies, which attract spiders and other insects, which are eaten by many birds. Nesting site for sparrows and buntings.	Strong clumps of foliage topped with showy, flat-topped or domed clusters of fragrant flowers. Pink, rose, lavender, or white flowers often have a contrasting-colored center. 3' to 4' tall.	Grow in full sun, in average-to-fertile, well-drained soil. Zones 4 to 8.
Smartweeds (*Polygonum* spp.)	Finches, sparrows, and other small birds eat oil-rich seeds.	Long-blooming spikes of pink or rosy red flowers top clumps of smooth foliage, which may turn red in fall. Various species range from a few inches to 6' tall.	Grow in partial to light shade, in moist soil rich in organic matter. Zones 3 to 8.

Quick Reference FAVORITE BERRY PLANTS FOR BIRDS

BERRIES attract a slew of birds, including gorgeous bright-colored tanagers, orioles, and grosbeaks. Here I've listed several of my favorite berry-producing plants for the bird garden. You'll find that adding berry plants to your landscape will give you beautiful, living bird feeders.

PLANT NAMES	BIRDS ATTRACTED	PLANT DESCRIPTION	CULTURE	COMMENTS
American cranberrybush (*Viburnum trilobum*)	Robins, thrushes, bluebirds, and many others	Rounded shrub to 12' tall, with three-lobed leaves; flat-topped clusters of white flowers in late spring; shining red fruits in early fall.	Grow in well-drained, moist soil, in sun to partial shade; irrigate during droughts. Zones 2 to 8.	Looks best planted as a hedge or a privacy screen.
Arrowwood (*Viburnum dentatum*)	A very wide range of berry-eating birds	Multistemmed shrub 8' to 15' tall. Clusters of small creamy flowers in early summer; oval blue-black fruits in fall.	Grow in well-drained soil, in sun to partial shade. Zones 2 to 8.	Buy in the fall, when you can see the fall color; only some plants turn rich red.
Barberries (*Berberis* spp.)	Catbirds, mockingbirds, and many others	Thorny, rounded shrubs varying from 18" to 6' tall. Yellow flowers are followed by bright red or orange berries.	Grow this adaptable, drought-tolerant shrub in well-drained soil in full sun. Zones 4 to 8.	Reddish purple-leaved cultivars like 'Crimson Velvet' or 'Helmond Pilla' add color to the garden.
Black currant (*Ribes nigrum*)	Robins, mockingbirds, jays, and many others	Twiggy shrub to 6' tall, with lobed leaves. Clusters of greenish white flowers followed by edible black fruits.	Grow in full sun to light shade, in well-drained soil. Zones 4 to 8.	Sale of currants is restricted in some states because they host white pine blister rust disease. Ask your extension agent about restrictions before planting.
Elderberries (*Sambucus* spp.)	A very wide range of berry-eating birds	6' to 10' multistemmed shrubs with white flowers and abundant clusters of tiny berries.	Grow in well-drained soil, in sun to part shade. Zones 4 to 8.	Try *S. canadensis*, the common garden variety with purple-black fruits, or grow American red elderberry (*S. pubens*).
Juneberries (*Amelanchier* spp.)	Waxwings, bluebirds, and many others	Shrubs or small trees with white flowers in early spring, followed by fruits that turn red, then blue-black or purple.	Grow in well-drained, moist, acid soil, in sun to shade. Zones 4 to 9 (some species are hardy to Zone 2).	'Autumn Brilliance' and 'Autumn Sunset' are graceful small trees; 'Prince William' is shrubby; 'Cumulus' grows 20' to 30' tall.
Strawberries (*Fragaria* spp. and hybrids)	Robins, catbirds, thrashers, and many others	Groundcovers with clumps of three-lobed leaves. White or pink flowers in spring followed by delectable red berries.	Grow in full sun in well-drained soil rich in organic matter. Zones 4 to 9.	Choose cultivars that you like, or try the tiny, sweet clusters of wild strawberry (*F. virginiana*).

FAVORITE NATIVE PLANTS FOR BIRDS

THE native plants you choose to grow will depend on where you live and the soil, light, and moisture conditions in your yard. Since I've gardened in Indiana, Pennsylvania, and Oregon, this selection of my favorite native plants for birds includes some from both East and West.

PLANT NAMES	BIRDS ATTRACTED	PLANT DESCRIPTION	NATIVE HABITAT	CULTURE AND COMMENTS
Blue flax (*Linum perenne*)	Goldfinches, house finches, purple finches, sparrows, and buntings eat the oil-rich seeds.	Delicate, wiry-stemmed perennial to 18" tall. Short, needlelike leaves; true blue flowers open in morning and close by afternoon.	Prairies and woods' edges east of the Cascade Mountains of Washington, Oregon, and California	Grow in sun, in any well-drained soil. Short-lived perennial that reseeds. Zones 5 to 10.
Buttonbush (*Cephalanthus occidentalis*)	Warblers, vireos, gnatcatchers, and orioles hunt insects among the flowers. Finches and buntings nest in the branches.	Deciduous shrub, 3' to 6' tall, but can grow 15' tall in the South. Pointed, oval leaves. Creamy powder puff–like flowers in summer are followed by balls of seeds that last through winter.	Marshes, ponds, and other wet sites from New Brunswick to Florida, and west to Minnesota and central California	Grow in moist or wet soil, in sun to shade. Combine with grasses or rushes to fill in for the twiggy-looking shrub in winter. Zones 5 to 10.
Crested iris (*Iris cristata*)	Native sparrows, thrushes, towhees, and other woodland birds can hide in foliage.	Perennial, 6" tall, with lavender blue flowers. Not a solid groundcover; it has spaces between tufts for birds to navigate freely.	Woodlands from Maryland south to Georgia, and west to Missouri	Grow in partial to full shade, in well-drained soil. Spreads rapidly by roots. Great for a shade garden. Zones 3 to 8.
Crossvine (*Bignonia capreolata*)	Hummingbirds drink nectar from the flowers. Catbirds may nest in the foliage.	High-climbing evergreen vine with long, pointed leaves that turn a rich bronze-maroon in winter. Clusters of trumpet-shaped flowers are dark orange outside, golden inside.	Woods and river bottoms, from Virginia to southern Illinois, and south to Florida and Louisiana	Grow in full sun to full shade, in moist, well-drained soil. Let it climb up a deciduous shade tree, where it can decorate the trunk in winter. Zones 6 to 9.
Desert marigold (*Baileya multiradiata*)	Native sparrows and finches eat the seeds.	Tender perennial grown as annual that forms tufts of gray foliage topped by stems of golden yellow, double-flowered daisies.	Mesas and dry plains in the Southwest and Mexico	Grow in full sun, in well-drained soil. Good naturalizer for dry gardens in the Southwest and Southern California.
Downy hawthorn (*Crataegus mollis*)	A wide variety of birds eat the fruits. Warblers and vireos eat insects when flowers are in bloom. Robins, and other birds may nest in the branches.	Deciduous tree, 20' to 30' tall, with a rounded, wide-spreading shape. Grayish bark, leaves are woolly when young, turning yellow to bronze red in fall. Strong-smelling clusters of white flowers in spring are followed by red fruits in late summer.	Woods' edges and hedgerows, from southern Ontario south to Virginia, west to South Dakota and Kansas	Grow in almost any soil, in sun to part shade. Makes an attractive small tree for a partly shady backyard. Zones 3 to 6.

Quick Reference	FAVORITE NATIVE PLANTS FOR BIRDS—CONTINUED			
PLANT NAMES	BIRDS ATTRACTED	PLANT DESCRIPTION	NATIVE HABITAT	CULTURE AND COMMENTS
Drummond's phlox, annual phlox (*Phlox drummondii*)	Hummingbirds visit flowers for nectar; flowers draw butterflies, which birds eat.	Annual that grows up to 18" tall, with clusters of red, pink, lavender, or white flowers in spring.	Open ground and grasslands in Texas	Grow in full sun, in well-drained soil. Self-sows. Plant in masses for best effect.
White fringe tree (*Chionanthus virginicus*)	Robins, thrushes, bluebirds, catbirds, orioles, thrashers, mockingbirds, waxwings, and tanagers eat the fruits.	Shrub or small tree up to 10'. Long, pointed, oblong leaves with slight gloss, and fleecy clouds of flowers in late spring to early summer. Hanging, small, dark blue, oval fruits are hidden by foliage.	Stream banks, edges of swamps, roadsides, or woods' edges from southern New Jersey to Florida, west to Texas	Grow in full sun to part shade, in moist, fertile soil. Also thrives in average garden soil. Easy to grow. Zones 3 to 9.
Giant four-o'clock (*Mirabilis multiflora*)	Hummingbirds come to flowers for nectar; the plant provides cover for wrens.	Perennial to 2' tall, spreading to 3' or wider, with tubular bright magenta flowers from late spring through summer.	Mountains or open grasslands of southern Colorado to Mexico, west to California	Grow in full sun, in sandy or otherwise very well-drained soil. Grow in a raised bed if you have heavy soil. Zones 5 to 9.
Hay-scented fern (*Dennstaedtia punctiloba*)	Towhees, quail, bobwhites, juncos, and other ground-dwelling birds take shelter and nest in the fronds.	Delicate, spring green lacy fronds spread by roots to cover a large area.	Woods' edges and clearings in eastern North America	Grow in sun to light shade, in moist, acid soil with plenty of organic matter. An excellent groundcover for an open woodland garden. Zones 4 to 8.
Indian blanket flower (*Gaillardia pulchella*)	Finches, buntings, and sparrows enjoy the seeds.	Drought-tolerant annual with downy leaves and 2" to 3" daisylike flowers.	Grasslands and open spaces from Florida to Colorado, south to Mexico	Grow in full sun, in any soil. Sow seeds in early spring for bloom in less than 2 months.
Possumhaw (*Ilex decidua*)	A wide variety of birds eat the fruits; native sparrows, towhees, and thrushes may nest in the plant.	Multistemmed shrub or small tree, 6' to 15' tall, with dense branches and beautiful glossy dark green leaves. Orange to red berries stud the branches in early fall.	Moist woods, from Virginia to Florida and west to Texas	Grow in full sun to partial shade in moist, acid soil high in organic matter. Excellent dense shrub for cover. Good for hedges. Zones 4 to 9.
Virginia sweetspire (*Itea virginica*)	All perching birds seek shelter in the evergreen foliage. Warblers, vireos, and orioles seek insects attracted to the flowers.	Evergreen shrub, usually 5' but can reach 10'. In shade, has upright form; in sun, wider and more densely branched with pointed, oval leaves. Spikes of tiny white, fragrant flowers open in summer, and mature to attractive seed spikes.	Streamsides and wet places from New Jersey to Florida, west to Missouri and Louisiana	Grow in sun to full shade in moist to average soil; also tolerates wet soil and drought. Plant near a path where you can enjoy the fragrant flowers. Zones 5 to 9.

FAVORITE EVERGREENS FOR BIRDS

HERE are eight favorite bird-attracting evergreens. (Keep in mind that hemlocks, hollies, junipers, and pines are also fabulous evergreens for birds.) Evergreens serve double duty in bird-friendly yards. They provide year-round shelter for birds, and their cones and berries are a great food source. And with such a varied list from which to choose, you're sure to find an evergreen that's perfect for your landscape.

PLANT NAMES	BIRDS ATTRACTED	PLANT DESCRIPTION	CULTURE
Balsam fir (*Abies balsamea*)	Nesting and roosting birds, including grosbeaks and robins; chickadees, juncos, jays, nuthatches, and other birds eat seeds	Narrow, upright trees, 40' to 60' tall, with rounded fragrant needles	Grows best in moist, acid soil in cool conditions. In warm areas, try Fraser fir (*A. fraseri*), which tolerates some heat. Zones 2 to 5.
Blue spruce (*Picea pungens*)	Nesting and roosting birds, especially grackles and house finches	150'-tall, cone-shaped tree with short, blue-gray needles	Plant in average, well-drained soil, in sun or light shade. Zones 2 to 7.
Box huckleberry (*Gaylussacia brachycera*)	Nesting and roosting birds, especially sparrows, towhees, and thrushes; catbirds, jays, thrushes, and waxwings eat fruits	Fine-textured, low-growing shrub that spreads slowly to form a large mat 6" to 18" high, with glossy leaves and blue-black berrylike fruits in late summer	Plant in fertile, moist, well-drained, acid soil, in partial shade. Zones 5 to 8.
Buckthorns (*Rhamnus cathartica*, *R. crocea*, and other spp.)	Nesting and roosting birds; catbirds, mockingbirds, and thrushes eat fruits	Spiny, dense shrub 3' to 10' tall, with dark, glossy green leaves and black or red berries	Grows in sun or shade, and can become invasive due to birds spreading seeds. Zones 2 to 9.
Douglas fir (*Pseudotsuga menziesii*)	Nesting and roosting birds	200'-tall, cone-shaped tree with soft needles and dangling, shaggy cones	Plant in sun to shade, in average, well-drained soil. Zones 4 to 6.
Japanese yew (*Taxus cuspidata*)	Nesting and roosting birds, especially doves and chipping sparrows; fruits eaten by mockingbirds, robins, and sparrows	15'-tall evergreen shrub with dense, soft-needled, green foliage in summer and green-black foliage and red fruits in winter	Plant in well-drained soil, in sun to shade. Zones 4 to 7.
Norway spruce (*Picea abies*)	Nesting and roosting birds, especially grackles and house finches	Tree tops out at 150' tall, with short, sharp-tipped needles and long, dangling cones	Plant in average, well-drained soil, in sun or shade. Zones 2 to 7.
Rhododendrons (*Rhododendron* spp.)	Nesting and roosting birds, and hummingbirds when flowering	Shrubs of 15' or more in height, with long, smooth leaves and clusters of showy flowers in spring	Plant in well-drained, acid soil, in sun or shade. Zones 4 to 7.

Quick Reference   FAVORITE GRASSES FOR BIRDS

DESPITE their delicate appearance, ornamental grasses are hardy plants that adapt to most parts of the country. No matter what size garden you have, there's a grass that's right for your garden and your bird friends. The grasses described below range in size from petite 1'-tall purple-top to towering 10' cattails. These grass plants shelter nests, and dry grass leaves are the perfect material for nest construction.

PLANT NAMES	BIRDS ATTRACTED	PLANT DESCRIPTION	CULTURE
Big bluestem (*Andropogon gerardii*)	Sparrows, meadowlarks, blackbirds, and other birds eat seeds. Sparrows and other ground-nesting birds build nests in the clumps.	Clumps grow 4' to 7' tall, with narrow foliage that emerges silvery blue in spring and turns bronze in winter. Branched seedheads look like a turkey's foot.	Plant in full sun in well-drained soil. Tolerates heat, humidity, and drought. Zones 4 to 10.
Common cattail (*Typha latifolia*)	Foliage shelters nests of red-winged and other blackbirds. Wrens, vireos, and chickadees pick fluff of ripened cattails to line their nests.	Coarse, strappy blades grow 6' to 10' tall, with equally tall stems topped by cigar-shaped, brown seedheads. Foliage turns yellow-brown in fall and winter.	Plant at water's edge or in water up to 12" deep, in full sun or part shade. Spreads rapidly. Zones 3 to 10.
Deer tongue grass (*Panicum clandestinum*)	Sparrows, finches, buntings, and other small birds enjoy seeds.	Forms low-growing clumps of bamboolike foliage with delicate sprays of seedheads at tips of arching stems. Foliage turns yellow in fall.	Plant in moist, humusy soil in shade. Zones 4 to 9.
Indian grass (*Sorghastrum nutans*)	Small birds forage below plants when ripe seeds drop.	2'- to 3'-tall clumps of grass with feathery wands of flowers rising 2' to 3' above strappy leaves. Foliage turns yellow to orange in fall.	Plant in sun to part shade. Tolerates drought, clay soil, wet soil, or dry soil. Zones 4 to 9.
Indian rice grass (*Orysopsis hymenoides*)	Many kinds of birds eagerly eat seeds.	1' to 2' tufts of narrow, delicate-looking foliage and many tall flower stems topped with delicate seedheads. Foliage is tan in summer, green in winter.	Plant in full sun in well-drained soil. Grows best in the arid West. Zones 8 to 10.
Little bluestem (*Schizachyrium scoparium*)	Birds take shelter and nest against clumps. Sparrows, juncos, and other small birds eat seeds.	Upright clumps grow 2' to 5' tall. Flower-topped stems emerge in summer, followed by fluffy plumes of seedheads. Foliage turns orange in fall and winter.	Plant in full sun; won't tolerate wet soils. Zones 3 to 10.
Purple-top (*Tridens flavus*)	Finches, sparrows, buntings, and other birds eat seeds. Foliage and old stems are popular nest material.	Low clumps of foliage grow to 1' or taller, with taller stems of drooping, red-purple flowers. Foliage turns tan in winter.	Plant in full sun to shade. Self-sows. Zones 5 to 9.
Switch grass (*Panicum virgatum*)	Native sparrows, juncos, and other birds eat seeds. Foliage is used for nest building.	Clumps of spiky foliage produce clouds of delicate flowers and seedheads that catch the light. Leaves turn ruddy red or golden in fall, beige in winter.	Plant in full sun. Grows well in most soils. Self-sows. Zones 5 to 9.

FAVORITE SHRUBS FOR BIRDS

CHOOSING shrubs for birds is difficult—not because there are few choices but because there are so many! This short listing is just a quick sampling of shrubs that offer shelter, nesting sites, and food for birds. You'll also find information on more great shrubs for birds, including viburnums, on page 140.

PLANT NAMES	BIRDS ATTRACTED	PLANT DESCRIPTION	CULTURE
Cotoneasters (*Cotoneaster* spp.)	Insect- and fruit-eating birds are lured by insect-attracting flowers and berries.	Species and cultivars vary from groundcover types to 10'- to 15'-tall shrubs; evergreen or semievergreen with bright red or black fruits.	Grows best in moist, well-drained soil; some tolerate dry soil; all need full sun. Most types hardy in Zones 3 to 7.
Gray dogwood (*Cornus racemosa*)	More than 100 species of birds are lured by insect-attracting flowers and berries; shelters roosting and nesting birds.	10'- to 15'-tall, multistemmed deciduous shrub with pointed, oval leaves, gray branches in summer; clusters of white berries on crimson stems in fall and winter.	Grows in wet and dry soil, in sun to full shade. Sprouts from the roots to form clumps. Zones 4 to 8.
Red osier dogwood (*Cornus sericea* [formerly *C. stolonifera*])	A wide range of birds is lured by insect-attracting flowers, berries, and nesting sites.	7'- to 9'-tall, multistemmed deciduous shrub with pointed, oval leaves that turn reddish purple in fall; deep red bark on young stems and clusters of white berries in winter.	Grows in almost any soil, including wet places, in full sun to shade. Spreads by underground stems. Zones 2 to 8.
Winged euonymus, burning bush (*Euonymus alata*)	Fruit-eating birds relish berries; many birds use it for nest sites and shelter.	10' or taller, deciduous shrub shaped like a large, flat-topped, mounded bush; brilliant red fall foliage; small dangling fruits have orange-red seed coats that peel away from red berries.	Thrives almost anywhere, except waterlogged soil, in sun to full shade. Zones 4 to 9.
Oregon grape holly (*Mahonia aquifolium*)	Insect- and fruit-eating birds are lured by insect-attracting flowers and berries; also offers shelter.	Evergreen 4'- to 6'-tall shrub with lustrous, hollylike leaves; clusters of bright yellow flowers; beautiful, blue-black berries.	Grows in moist, well-drained, acid soil; grows best in partial to full shade but tolerates sun if protected from drying winds. Zones 4 to 8.
Common privet (*Ligustrum vulgare*)	Insect-eating birds are lured to insect-attracting flowers; provides shelter and nest sites.	Dense, semievergreen shrub 12' or taller, with small, leathery, dark green leaves and creamy flowers with strong aroma; birds ignore the shrub's black berries.	Grows almost anywhere, except wet soil, in sun to shade. Zones 4 to 7.
Weigela (*Weigela florida*)	Nectar-rich flowers attract hummingbirds; many birds use it for nesting sites.	Deciduous shrub, 6' to 9' tall, forms a wide, arching mound, with trumpet-shaped pink or red flowers in summer. Best grown in hedges because of its undistinguished shape.	Grows in well-drained soil, in full sun. Zones 4 to 9.

BACKYARD BIRDS AT A GLANCE

Here's a handy reference guide to help you identify birds that visit your yard and gardens—as well as the scoop on their favorite foods. Chances are, you probably see many of the 42 birds listed here on a regular basis. But if you don't, you'll also find tips on what you can do to invite those birds that you may not see very frequently—but would like to—into your backyard. For example, planting conifers—such as spruces or hemlocks—is a great way to entice crossbills to your yard. Orioles, on the other hand, are drawn to cherries and strawberries. Follow the suggestions, and you'll be able to sit back and enjoy the host of feathered friends that become regulars at your feeders.

KEY 🐦 Description 🖼 Favorite foods 🏠 Inviting them in

BLACKBIRDS

🐦 Blackbirds are medium to large birds, ranging from just under robin size to as big as a blue jay, with fairly long, sharp beaks and a loudmouth habit.

🖼 Cracked corn, millet, smartweed, and ragweed seeds

Other favorite foods:
• Apples
• Blueberries
• Bread
• Nuts
• Raisins
• Suet
• Sunflower seeds

🏠 A backyard pond or marshy area makes a perfect nesting spot for these birds.

BLUEBIRDS

🐦 Bluebirds have straight, pointed bills and are about 7 inches long. Both males and females are blue, but male birds have brilliant blue feathers, whereas females have duller, blue-gray feathers.

🖼 Mostly insects, as well as berries and other small fruit

Other favorite foods:
• Mealworms
• Peanut butter
• Raisins
• Sunflower hearts

🏠 Bluebirds appreciate a nice nest box to replace the holes in dead trees and wooden fence posts that were once their homes of choice.

(continued)

KEY   ◀ Description   📷 Favorite foods   🐦 Inviting them in

BUNTINGS

◀ Buntings are just 4½ inches long. Their feathers are vivid sapphire blue, turquoise, and chestnut, or a rainbow of blue, red, yellow, and green.

📷 Seeds are their primary food, particularly the seeds of dandelion, lamb's-quarters, smartweed, goldenrod, and asters. They also like millet.

Other favorite foods:
- Canary seed
- Chopped nuts
- Chopped peanuts
- Rapeseed

🐦 Be sure your yard includes shrubs, hedges, and the brushy, weedy areas that buntings prefer.

CARDINALS

◀ Male cardinals have rich red feathers and a snazzy black mast, while females have buffy brown feathers with splashes of orange-red on their crest, wings, and tail.

📷 Sunflower and safflower seeds, cracked corn, weed seeds, fruit, elm buds, and a variety of insects

Other favorite foods:
- Bread
- Peanuts
- Suet

🐦 Cardinals like a yard with lots of shrubs for cover, where they can safely move through corridors of hedges or shrubbery.

CATBIRDS

◀ Both males and females are dark gray with a black cap and a patch of rich deep chestnut beneath the base of the tail. Adult birds are about 8½ inches long.

📷 Beetles, grasshoppers, and other insects, as well as berries

Other favorite foods:
- Bread
- Cereal
- Crackers
- Peanuts
- Raisins

🐦 Catbirds like to nest in leafy shrubs, such as honeysuckle, weigela, and lilacs.

CHICKADEES

◀ All chickadees are about 4 to 5 inches long and have a snazzy dark cap and black bib with white cheek patches. Males and females look alike.

📷 Sunflower seed, chick scratch, peanut butter, doughnuts, and suet

Other favorite foods:
- Acorns
- Baked goods
- Bread
- Mealworms
- Peanuts
- Pine nuts

🐦 Chickadees are attracted to gardens with trees where they can glean insects, larvae, and insect eggs.

CROSSBILLS

Male crossbills are reddish birds about 5 to 6½ inches long. The females are dusky yellowish green. The upper and lower parts of their beaks overlap at an angle.

Sunflower seeds; they also like salt

Other favorite foods:
- Pine nuts

Planting conifers is the surest way to attract crossbills to your yard. Pines, spruces, hemlocks, firs, and larches are all good choices.

CUCKOOS

Cuckoos are slim, streamlined birds, almost a foot long from the tip of their down-curved beak to the end of their long tail. They have brown backs and snowy white bellies; males and females look alike.

Leaf-eating caterpillars, other insects, and fruit

Other favorite foods:
- Mulberries
- Raspberries

Planting plenty of shrubs and trees will invite cuckoos to your yard. You can also plant mulberries, raspberries, and grapes to attract them.

DOVES

Doves are large birds, about 12 to 14 inches long, with a small head atop a plump-breasted body. Male doves are decorated with iridescent color on their necks that glow with metallic green, purple, or pink in the sun.

Millet, grass seed, and corn

Other favorite foods:
- Acorns
- Bread
- Buckwheat
- Elderberries
- Nuts

Water is a big draw for doves. The like a ground-level pool or shallow basin for drinking and bathing.

FLICKERS

Flickers are big brown woodpeckers—about 12 inches long—with a dashing black crescent across their chest and vividly colored underwings.

Suet, bread, raisins, ants, lawn grubs, and grasshoppers

Other favorite foods:
- Amelanchier berries
- Blueberries
- Grass seed
- Peanut butter
- Watermelon

Flickers enjoy all kinds of berries, so planting berry bushes or other fruiting shrubs is a good way to attract these show birds to your yard.

(continued)

KEY   ◀ Description   📷 Favorite foods   🏠 Inviting them in

GOLDFINCHES

◀ Males are 5 inches long and have buttery yellow bodies with gleaming black wings accented by white bars, with a touch of black on their heads. Females are soft olive green and subdued yellow.

📷 Black oil sunflower seed, niger seed, and seeds of a wide variety of common garden plants, including zinnias and coneflowers.

Other favorite foods:
• Canary seed

🏠 Water is a big draw for goldfinches, who like to bathe daily. They prefer a low, wide, shallow bath to splash in and sip from, although they'll also use pedestal-type birdbaths.

GROSBEAKS

◀ Grosbeaks are the size of a cardinal and come in different shades of yellow, orange, blue, red-pink, and brown.

📷 Seeds and berries

Other favorite foods:
• Acorns
• Cherries
• Common ragweed
• Corn
• Crackers
• Wheat
• Wild grapes

🏠 Plant grosbeaks' favorite berry bushes: bittersweet, blackberries, elderberries, and barberries.

GRACKLES

◀ Grackles have glossy black plumage with a sheen of purple, green, bronze, or blue, depending on the species and the light. Their tails are long and sweep the ground like the train of Cinderella's gown. Some species of grackles are as large as 16 inches.

📷 Cracked corn, bread, grubs, beetles, grasshoppers, and armyworms

Other favorite foods:
• Apples

🏠 A patch of lawn grass is all the invitation grackles need to visit your backyard. They like open spaces, usually near water.

HOUSE FINCHES

◀ Female house finches are evenly streaked in brown over their entire bodies; males have light, strawberry red color on their head and upper breast, while the rest of their body is a streaky brown.

📷 Sunflower, millet, niger seeds, tree buds, berries

Other favorite foods:
• Bread crumbs
• Crushed eggshells
• Nectar
• Salt

🏠 A yard full of dandelions is heaven to finches, who devour the little seeds at the ends of the silky "parachutes."

HUMMINGBIRDS

Hummingbirds come in gorgeous shades of green, bronze, purple, blue, red, pink, and orange. Males are the beauties, with females being mostly green above and whitish below.

Nectar, small insects, small spiders

Other favorite foods:
• Sap

In addition to hanging up a sugar-water feeder, plant some flowers to entice these birds. The best flowers for hummers have tubular blossoms, like honeysuckle, salvias, and bee balm.

JAYS

With a length approaching 12 inches, jays are hard to overlook. Most jays are shades of blue, although in certain areas of the country you can also find a gray-feathered jay.

Sunflower seeds, peanuts, nuts, corn, bread, dog food, chick scratch, chopped suet

Other favorite foods:
• Acorns
• Crackers

Plant nut trees, such as oaks, beeches, pecans, and walnuts, as well as berry plants, such as sumac, blueberries, grapes, cherries, and serviceberries.

JUNCOS

Juncos have distinct whitish pink beaks that stand out against their faces. They're small—5 to 6 inches long—with white outer tail feathers. Female juncos are a bit paler than males.

Millet and finely chopped suet

Other favorite foods:
• Birdseed mix
• Bread crumbs
• Cracker crumbs
• Grass seed
• Peanut butter
• Pine nuts

Juncos like the seeds of cosmos, zinnias, and tickseed sunflower (*Bidens aristosa*).

KILLDEERS

Killdeers are robin size, but with long legs. They have dark stripes on their head and neck; their back and wings are gray-brown and their underparts are pure white. When they fly, killdeers reveal an otherwise hidden patch of rich deep orange just above their black-and-white-tipped tail feathers.

Insects, particularly grubs and earthworms

Other favorite foods:
• Grasshoppers
• Beetles

Killdeers like open areas of lawn where they can search for grubs and earthworms.

(continued)

KEY   ◢ Description   ◢ Favorite foods   ◢ Inviting them in

KINGLETS

◢ These birds just top the 3-inch mark from tip of beak to end of tail. They have gray-green bodies and two white wing bars. Ruby-crowned kinglets have a bright red patch on the top of their heads, and golden-crowned kinglets have a dash of butter yellow.

◢ Insects

Other favorite foods:
- Nectar
- Raw hamburger
- Suet
- Sumac berries

◢ Plant insect-harboring trees such as hemlocks, spruces, oaks, and pines.

MAGPIES

◢ From tip to tail, magpies measure 16 to 18 inches long; their tails alone can be 12 inches long. They're colored in a striking black-and-white pattern with iridescent greenish black tail feathers and greenish blue upper wings.

◢ Grasshoppers, crickets, ground beetles, some fruit

Other favorite foods:
- Apples
- Cereal
- Corn
- Figs
- Suet

◢ Magpies love lunchmeat, bread, and other leftover treats.

MARTINS

◢ Purple martins aren't purple at all: They're glossy deep blue, almost black, with a forked tail. Females and juvenile birds have light bellies.

◢ Insects, including flies, mosquitoes, moths, and cucumber beetles

Other favorite foods:
- Ants
- Butterflies
- Dragonflies
- Mealworms

◢ Scatter crushed eggshells on the ground below their house, or in another open area where they're easily accessible.

MEADOWLARKS

◢ Meadowlarks are about $8\frac{1}{2}$ inches long and shaped like starlings, with chunky bodies, stubby tails, and short legs. They have shining golden yellow breasts, slashed with a broad black V across the chest. Their backs are streaky brown.

◢ Insects, birdseed, cracked corn, wheat, oats, and millet

Other favorite foods:
- Crickets
- Cutworms
- Grasshoppers

◢ A meadow garden may attract a meadowlark, especially if your yard is near farm fields or pastureland.

MOCKINGBIRDS

Mockingbirds are streamlined gray birds up to 9 inches long with white undersides and flashy white wing patches and outer tail feathers. Males and females look alike.

Corn, chopped suet, millet, grapes, raisins, dog food

Other favorite foods:
- Bread
- Cereal
- Mealworms

Mockingbirds are big fruit eaters, so elderberries, hollies, mulberries, raspberries and other brambles, and many other fruiting plants will bring them to your garden.

NUTHATCHES

These dapper little birds are dressed in blue gray above, white beneath. Head markings vary depending on the species. Males and females look alike.

Corn, nuts, suet and sunflower seeds

Other favorite foods:
- Elderberries
- Milo
- Peanut butter
- Rapeseed
- Wheat

Plant conifers and nut trees in your yard. Nuthatches help keep trees healthy by eating tons of beetles, caterpillars, wood borers, and other insects.

ORIOLES

Male orioles are decked out in brilliant orange or bright yellow with gleaming black hoods, wings, and tails. Females are dressed in greenish garb, washed with a hint of yellow or pale orange.

Orange halves, homemade nectar, and suet

Other favorite foods:
- Apples
- Corn
- Figs
- Peas

To make your yard more tempting to orioles, plant blackberries, cherries, elderberries, mulberries, strawberries, and figs.

PHOEBES

Phoebes have medium-size, slim beaks and longish tails. They're about 6 inches long, and males and females look alike.

Beetles, flies, moths, and other bugs

Other favorite foods:
- Bayberries
- Hollies

The seeds in your feeders won't interest phoebes, but plentiful bug life will. If you grow a wide variety of flowering plants and you have a water source available, you'll encourage phoebes to visit.

(continued)

BACKYARD BIRDS AT A GLANCE—CONTINUED

KEY ◄ Description 🖼 Favorite foods 🏠 Inviting them in

ROBINS

◄ This familiar bird, with its ruddy orange-red breast and gray-brown back, is about 8½ inches long. Female birds have a paler belly than the males, and during nesting season they may show a bald patch on the breast.

🖼 Corn, raisins, bread, and chopped suet

Other favorite foods:
- Apples
- Crackers
- Mealworms

🏠 Make your yard inviting for robins by adding bayberry, elderberry, grape, crabapple, and other fruit-producing shrubs and trees.

SISKINS

◄ These tame backyard birds are 4 inches long with streaky brown feathers and patches of yellow in each wing and at the base of the tail.

🖼 Millet, nectar, niger, and sunflower seeds

Other favorite foods:
- Bachelor's button seed
- Birdseed mix
- Canary mix
- Cosmos seeds
- Zinnia seeds

🏠 Leave a patch of weeds like lamb's-quarters standing in winter. In spring, gone-to-seed dandelions will draw migrating birds.

SAPSUCKERS

◄ Sapsuckers are moderate-size woodpeckers, about 7½ to 8½ inches long. Seen from the back, they look mostly black—they don't have the black-and-white markings of the more familiar downy and hairy woodpeckers. Both male and female yellow-bellied sapsuckers have a red patch on the crown of their black-and-white-striped head; males also have a red throat.

🖼 Suet and nectar

Other favorite food:
- Sunflower seeds

🏠 Sapsuckers love a sweet treat, so tempt them with jelly doughnuts hung by a string.

SPARROWS

◄ Most sparrows are small, streaky brown birds, about 4½ to 5½ inches long. Males and females look alike.

🖼 Corn, millet, milo, and suet

Other favorite foods:
- Birdseed mix
- Bread crumbs
- Cereal
- Crackers

🏠 Leave a weedy or unmown grassy area in a corner of your yard to shelter a variety of sparrows. They'll peck at pigweed, goldenrod, ragweed, foxtail grass, and other common weeds, from the time the seeds ripen on through winter.

SWIFTS

Swifts are from 5 to 7 inches long, but their wingspan is about 1 foot. Chimney swifts are deep gray; white-throated swifts have striking white markings on their sides and throat; Vaux's swift looks like a chimney swift with lighter-colored underparts.

Insects

Other favorite food:
- Mosquitoes

Other than the insects in the air in your yard, the only thing that will attract them is a hospitable chimney in which to build their nests.

TANAGERS

Tanagers have large but thin and pointed beaks. These birds range from 6 to 7 inches long. Most male tanagers are some shade of red, with the exception of the western tanager, which has a bright red head, yellow body, and black wings and tail. Female tanagers are olive drab fading to yellow.

Bread, doughnuts, mealworms, and chopped bananas

Other favorite food:
- Peanut butter

Tanagers enjoy fruit, so plant grapes, cherries, mulberries, serviceberries, Virginia creeper, and dogwoods to attract them in fall.

THRASHERS

These birds are big—about 10 inches long—and range in color from brown to grayish tan, depending on the species.

Bread crumbs, corn, and suet

Other favorite foods:
- Apples
- Baked goods
- Cactus fruits
- Cooked pasta
- Grapes
- Leftovers
- Meat scraps
- Nuts

Attract thrashes to your backyard with berry plants, such as hollies, brambles, and blueberries.

THRUSHES

Thrushes are robin-size birds of varying hues of brown (the exception is the gold-and-blue variety thrush). They have snowy white bellies freckled at the throat and breast with dark brown spots. Males and females look alike.

Birdseed mix, berries, fruit, millet, and chopped suet

Other favorite foods:
- Figs
- Mealworms
- Peanut butter
- Raisins

Entice thrushes to your yard by providing plenty of cover. Also fill your garden with berried trees and shrubs.

(continued)

KEY ◀ Description 🐦 Favorite foods 🦅 Inviting them in

TITMICE

◀ Titmice are gray birds with paler bellies, often blushed with pink at the sides. These 4½- to 5½-inch birds also wear a jazzy crest atop their bright-eyed heads. Males and females look alike.

🐦 Sunflower seeds, suet, peanuts, and bread

Other favorite foods:
- Acorns
- Apples
- Baked goods
- Cereal
- Corn

🦅 Plant berry-bearing shrubs, such as bayberries, sumac, serviceberries, brambles, blueberries, and wild cherries.

TOWHEES

◀ Towhees are actually giant-size sparrows. These 6- to more than 7-inch-long birds have long tails with rounded tips. Males are either warm buffy brown, grayish, or tricolored. Females are brown with streaky underparts.

🐦 Birdseed mix, corn, and chopped suet

Other favorite foods:
- Acorns
- Baked goods

🦅 Offer towhees crumbled bread, millet, chicken scratch, and wheat or oats. Fruit and berries will also lure them to your yard.

VIREOS

◀ Vireos are sleek greenish birds ranging from 4 to 5 inches long, depending on species. Their bellies are paler than their backs, often with touches of yellow or white that blend into the green. Females and males look alike.

🐦 Insects and berries

Other favorite foods:
- Beetles
- Caterpillars

🦅 A garden with plenty of trees and shrubs will draw vireos, especially during migration time in spring and fall. Vireos find mulberries and wild cherries particularly irresistible.

WARBLERS

◀ Warblers are small birds, many of them measuring about 4½ inches from beak to tail tip. Most are dressed in olive or yellow plumage, with various colorful accents—head caps, eye stripes, wing bars, tail patches—on the males and more subtle variations of these trademarks among the females. Most of the males are decorated with flashy splashes of orange, blue, chestnut, or black.

🐦 Figs and suet

Other favorite food:
- Sumac berries

🦅 A yard filled with vegetation or spring-flowering trees like crabapples is a great draw.

WAXWINGS

- Waxwings are soft shades of fawn, gray, or tawny brown, with a bright yellow band at the tip of the tail. They have a striking black mask and chin bib, as well as a jaunty pointed crest. Males and females look alike. Cedar waxwings are about 6 inches long, while Bohemian waxwings are bigger.

- Berries

Other favorite food:
  - Cherries

- Attract these bird to your yard with berry bushes and fruit trees. They enjoy cherries, elderberries, mulberries, crabapples, hollies, hawthorns, and just about any other kind of fruit or berry.

WRENS

- These little brown birds have faintly barred backs or wings and jaunty tails.

- Bread crumbs, mealworms, and suet

Other favorite foods:
  - Apples
  - Baked goods
  - Meat scraps
  - Peanut butter

- A yard with plenty of shrubs, annuals, and perennials, along with brambles, elderberries, or other small, soft fruits is wren haven.

WOODPECKERS

- Male and female woodpeckers generally look alike, except for the male's head markings. Size varies with species, from the $5\frac{3}{4}$-inch downy woodpecker to the 15-inch pileated woodpecker. Black-and-white wing stripes are common on many species. On many woodpeckers, the wing stripes extend across their backs, an effect called ladder-backed.

- Sunflower seeds, corn, and nuts

Other favorite foods:
  - Acorns
  - Figs

- Many woodpeckers are fond of fruit and will visit mulberry and cherry trees.

YELLOWTHROATS

- Males and females are olive green on top and yellow beneath; the male has a sporty black mask across his face. The male's belly is bright buttercup yellow; the female is paler.

- Insects

Other favorite food:
  - Sunflower seeds

- A densely planted perennial garden will attract yellowthroats for both dining pleasure and raising a family.

Resources and Recommended Reading

BIRD-FEEDING SUPPLIES

The ever-growing popularity of bird feeding means that sources of feeders, food, and other bird-related items abound. Your best source of supplies may be your local garden center or wild-bird specialty shop, but you'll also find bird feeders and birdhouses at most discount stores and hardware stores. Feed mills are a great source of low-cost birdseed and grains if you buy in large quantity. Fast-dissolving superfine sugar, which melts instantly even in cold water and is great for making nectar, is available at some supermarkets or from restaurant- and bar-supply shops.

Many cottage-industry bird box and feeder makers have entered the market. Check the back pages of any bird or wildlife magazine (see page 207 for listings) for advertisements and places to send for catalogs. You may also want to shop for supplies from the mail-order firms listed here.

Arundale Products
P.O. Box 4637
St. Louis, MO 63108
Phone: (800) 866-2473
Web site:
   www.skycafe.com/main.html
Squirrel-proof bird feeders

The Audubon Workshop
5200 Schenley Place
Lawrenceburg, IN 47025
Phone: (812) 537-3583

Bill Chandler Farms
R.R. 2
Noble, IL 62868
Phone: (800) 752-2473
Birdseed in bulk

Down to Earth
4 Highland Circle
Lucas, TX 75002
Phone: (800) 865-1996
Fax: (972) 442-2816
E-mail: info@downtoearth.com
Web site: www.downtoearth.com
Simple cypress-wood houses and wonderful see-through bird feeders and birdhouses that you can attach to windows

Droll Yankees, Inc.
27 Mill Road
Foster, RI 02825
Phone: (800) 352-9164
Fax: (401) 647-7620
E-mail: custserv@drollyankees.com
Web site: www.drollyankees.com

Duncraft, Inc.
102 Fisherville Road
Concord, NH 03303-2086
Phone: (800) 593-5656
Fax: (603) 226-3735
E-mail: info@duncraft.com
Web site: www.duncraft.com

Nature's Way
P.O. Box 188
Ross, OH 45061
Phone: (800) 318-2611
Fax: (513) 737-5421
Web site: www.thenature'sway.com

Plow & Hearth
P.O. Box 6000
Madison, VA 22727
Phone: (800) 627-1712
Fax: (800) 843-2509
Web site: www.plowhearth.com

Wellscroft Farm Fence Systems
167 Sunset Hill-Chesham
Harrisville, NH 03450
Phone: (603) 827-3464
Fax: (603) 827-3666

Wild Bird Centers of America, Inc.
Phone: (800) 945-3247 (to locate a store near you)
Web site: www.wildbirdcenter.com

Wild Birds Unlimited
11711 North College Avenue
Suite 146
Carmel, IN 46032
Phone: (888) 302-2473
Fax: (317) 571-7110
Web site: www.wbu.com
Tips for feeding and housing birds

**Wild Wings Organic Wild Bird
  Foods**
220 Congress Park Drive #232
Delray Beach, FL 33445
Phone: (800) 346-0269
E-mail: wildwings@aol.com
Web site: www.wildwings
  organic.com
Certified organic bird foods

ORGANIZATIONS

American Bird Conservancy
1250 24th Street NW, Suite 400
Washington, DC 20037
E-mail: abc@abcbirds.org
Web site: www.abcbirds.org
*A nonprofit organization that builds
coalitions of conservation groups,
scientists, and the public in order to
identify and protect important sites for
bird conservation; annual membership fee
includes ABC's quarterly magazine
about bird conservation and a newsletter
on policy issues affecting birds*

The American Birding Association
P.O. Box 6599
Colorado Springs, CO 80934
Phone: (800) 850-2473;
  (719) 578-9703
Fax: (719) 578-1480
Web site: www.americanbirding.org
*Contributes to bird conservation and aids
birders in gaining knowledge and skills*

**Backyard Wildlife Habitat
  Program**
National Wildlife Federation
11100 Wildlife Center Drive
Reston, VA 20190-5362
Phone: (703) 438-6000
Web site: www.nwf.org
*Free information on developing a bird-
friendly backyard; provide a certificate if
you follow through*

**The Cornell Laboratory
  of Ornithology**
159 Sapsucker Woods Road
Ithaca, NY 14850
Phone (800) 843-BIRD (2473)
Fax: (607) 254-2415
Web site:
  www.birds.cornell.edu/PFW
*Project Feeder Watch; the Great Back-
yard Bird Count; lists of birds common to
different areas*

The Hummingbird Society
P.O. Box 394
Newark, DE 19715
Phone: (302) 369-3699;
  (800) 529-3699
Fax: (302) 369-1816
Web site: www.hummingbird.org

National Audubon Society
700 Broadway
New York, NY 10003
Phone: (212) 979-3000
Fax: (212) 979-3188
Web site: www.audubon.org
*Founded in 1905, one of the biggest
nonprofit conservation organizations
and is active worldwide in all kinds of
conservation issues as well as birds; join
a local branch to meet other birders,
participate in bird counts, and enjoy other
bird-related activities*

National Bird-Feeding Society
P.O. Box 23L
Northbrook, IL 60065-0023
Phone: (847) 272-0135
Fax: (847) 498-4092
Web site: www.birdfeeding.org
*Organization devoted to bird feeding;
annual fee includes bi-monthly newsletter
and other information on bird feeding*

National Wildlife Health Center
6006 Schroeder Road
Madison, WI 53711
Phone: (608) 270-2400
Fax: (608) 270-2415
Web site:
  www.nwhc.usgs.gov

The Nature Conservancy
4245 North Fairfax Drive
Suite 100
Arlington, VA 22203
Phone: (800) 628-6860
Fax: (703) 841-1283
Web site: www.tnc.org

North American Rare Bird Alert (NARBA)
P.O. Box 6599
Colorado Springs, CO 80934
Phone: (719) 578-9703
Web site: www.americanbirding.org
    (go to the Rare Bird Alert link)

North American Bird Banding Program
For U.S. residents, contact:
Bird Banding Laboratory
U.S. Geological Survey—
    Biological Resources Division
Patuxent Wildlife Research Center
12100 Beech Forest Road
    Suite 4037
Laurel, MD 20708-4037
Phone: (301) 497-5790
Fax: (301) 497-5784
E-mail: BBL@mail.fws.gov
Web site: www.mbr-
    pwrc.usgs.gov/bbl/bbl.htm
For Canadian residents, contact:
Bird Banding Office
National Wildlife Research Centre
Canadian Wildlife Service
Hull, Quebec, Canada K1A 0H3
Phone: (819) 994-6176
Fax: (819) 953-6612
Learn how to create your own banding research program or volunteer with other banders

The North American Bluebird Society
P.O. Box 74
Darlington, WI 53530
Phone: (888) 235-1331
Web site:
    www.nabluebirdsociety.org
Advice on how to contribute to bluebird recovery

Purple Martin Conservation Association
Edinboro University of
    Pennsylvania
Edinboro, PA 16444
Phone: (814) 734-4420
Fax: (814) 734-5803
Web site: www.purplemartin.org

Songbird Foundation
2367 Eastlake Avenue East
Seattle, WA 98102
Phone: (206) 374-3674
Fax: (206) 374-3675
E-mail: kim@songbird.org
Web site: www.songbird.org
Nonprofit group working to raise awareness about the negative impact of sun-grown coffee production on songbird habitat; funds projects that promote shade-grown/organic coffee growing

U.S. Department of Agriculture
14th & Independence Avenue SW
Washington, DC 20250
Phone: (202) 720-2791
Fax: (202) 720-2166
Web site: www.fsa.usda.gov/edso
    (for state agencies) and
    www.usda.gov/news/garden/htm
    (for gardening info)

SOURCES OF SEEDS AND PLANTS

When you shop for plants, visit local nurseries that grow their own plants or buy from mail-order firms. Plants from discount stores often haven't been cared for properly and may not establish themselves as well in your garden. Some mail-order companies charge a small fee for their catalogs; you'll often get a credit on your first order.

The following is just a small selection of mail-order nurseries. Ask gardening friends what companies they recommend, too.

NATIVE PLANTS

Busse Gardens
17160 245th Avenue
Big Lake, MN 55309
Phone: (800) 544-3192
Fax: (763) 263-1473
E-mail: customerservice@
    bussegardens.com
Reliable and beautiful perennial plants that can take cold but also thrive in milder gardens

Comstock Seed
917 Highway 88
Gardenerville, NV 89410
Phone: (775) 746-3681
Fax: (775) 746-1701
Web site: www.comstockseed.com
Seeds of drought-tolerant native grasses and plants of the Great Basin

Edible Landscaping
P.O. Box 77
Afton, VA 22920-0077
Phone: (434) 361-9134
Fax: (434) 361-1916
Web site: www.eat-it.com
Plants for you and the birds (and other wildlife); lots of fruit-bearing trees and shrubs

Finch Blueberry Nursery
P.O. Box 699
Bailey, NC 27807
Phone: (252) 235-4664
Web site: www.danfinch.com
Wide selection of blueberries for your bird garden

Forestfarm
990 Tetherow Road
Williams, OR 97544-9599
Phone: (541) 846-7269
Fax: (541) 846-6963
Web site: www.forestfarm.com
More than 2,000 plants, including wildflowers, perennials, and an outstanding variety of trees and shrubs

Kurt Bluemel, Inc.
2740 Greene Lane
Baldwin, MD 21013-9523
Phone: (800) 248-PLUG (7584)
Fax: (410) 557-9785
Web site: www.kurtbluemel.com
Ornamental grasses

Niche Gardens
1111 Dawson Road
Chapel Hill, NC 27516
Phone: (919) 967-0078
Fax: (919) 967-4026
Web site: www.nichegdn.com
Generous-size plants of grasses, nursery-propagated wildflowers, perennials, and herbs

Plant Delights Nusery
9241 Sauls Road
Raleigh, NC 27603
Phone: (919) 772-4794
Fax: (919) 662-0370
Web site: www.plantdelights.com
A broad and eclectic selection of new and unusual perennials, along with many old favorites; many natives

Plants of the Southwest
3095 Agua Fria Road
Route 6, Box 11A
Santa Fe, NM 87507
Phone: (800) 788-7333;
    (505) 438-8888
Web site:
    www.plantsofthesouthwest.com
Drought-tolerant native plants and seeds

Prairie Moon Nursery
Route 3, Box 163
Winona, MN 55987
Phone: (507) 452-1362
Fax: (507) 454-5238
Web site: www.prairiemoon
    nursery.com
An outstanding variety of native prairie grasses and wildflowers; also lots of seeds

Prairie Nursery, Inc.
P.O. Box 306
Westfield, WI 53964
Phone: (800) 476-9453
Fax: (608) 296-2741
Web site: www.prairienursery.com
An excellent source of native wildflowers and grasses, many of them ideal for bird gardens

Raintree Nursery
391 Butts Road
Morton, WA 98536-9700
Phone: (360) 496-6400
Fax: (888) 770-8358
Web site: www.raintreenursery.com
A wide selection of fruit trees and shrubs

Sunlight Gardens, Inc.
174 Golden Lane
Andersonville, TN 37705
Phone: (865) 494-8237
Fax: (865) 494-7086
E-mail: sungardens@aol.com
Terrific selection of wildflowers, all nursery propagated, of southeastern and northeastern North America

Tripple Brook Farm
37 Middle Road
Southampton, MA 01073
Phone: (413) 527-4626
Fax: (413) 527-9853
Web site:
    www.tripplebrookfarm.com
Lively catalog of wildflowers and other northeastern native plants, plus fruits and shrubs

We-Du Nurseries
2055 Polly Spout Road
Marion, NC 28752
Phone: (828) 738-8300
Fax: (828) 738-8131
Web site: www.we-du.com
Impressive selection of wildflowers and perennials, including lots of woodland plants

Wildlife Nurseries
P.O. Box 2724
Oshkosh, WI 54903-2724
Phone: (920) 231-3780
Fax: (920) 231-3554
Excellent, informative listing of plants and seeds of native grasses, annuals, and perennials that attract birds and other wildlife; also water garden plants and supplies

Woodlanders, Inc.
1128 Colleton Avenue
Aiken, SC 29801
Phone/fax: (803) 648-7522
Web site: www.woodlanders.com
A fantastic collection of native trees, shrubs, ferns, vines, and perennials, plus other good garden plants. It's a list only, no pictures or descriptions, so if you're a newcomer to plants, pull out a plant encyclopedia to consult as you go.

NATIVE ROSES

Forestfarm
990 Tetherow Road
Williams, OR 97544-9599
Phone: (541) 846-7269
Web site: www.forestfarm.com

Hortico, Inc.
723 Robson Road, R.R #1
Waterdown, Ontario, Canada
    LOR 2H1
Phone: (905) 689-6984;
    (905) 689-3002
Fax: (905) 689-6566
Web site: www.hortico.com

The Roseraie at Granite Ridge
3202 Friendship Road
Waldoboro, ME 04572-0919
Phone: (207) 832-6330
Fax: (800) 933-4508
Web site: www.roseraie.com

WATER GARDEN PLANTS AND SUPPLIES

Lilypons Water Gardens
6800 Lilipons Road
P.O. Box 10
Buckeystown, MD 21717-0010
Phone: (800) 999-5459
Fax: (800) 879-5459
Web site: www.lilypons.com

Van Ness Water Gardens
2460 North Euclid Avenue
Upland, CA 91784-1199
Phone: (909) 982-2425
Fax: (909) 949-7217
Web site: www.vng.com

William Tricker, Inc.
7125 Tanglewood Drive
Independence, OH 44131
Phone: (800) 524-3492
Fax: (216) 524-6688
Web site: www.tricker.com
Perennial water garden specialist; plants, books, and water-garden-care products

BOOKS

Adams, George. *Birdscaping Your Garden.* Emmaus, PA: Rodale, 1998.

Barnes, Thomas G. *Gardening for the Birds.* Lexington, KY: University Press of Kentucky, 1999.

Burton, Robert. *National Audubon Society's North American Birdfeeder Handbook.* Rev. ed. New York: DK Publishing, 1995.

Ellis, Barbara. *Attracting Birds and Butterflies: How to Plan and Plant a Backyard Habitat.* Taylor's Weekend Gardening Guides. New York: Houghton Mifflin, 1997.

Harrison, George H. *Garden Birds of America: A Gallery of Garden Birds and How to Attract Them.* Minocqua, WI: Willow Creek Press, 1996.

Kress, Stephen W. *National Audubon Society: The Bird Garden.* New York: DK Publishing, 1995.

National Audubon Society. *The Audubon Society Handbook for Birders.* New York: Charles Scribner's Sons, 1981.

Proctor, Noble. *Garden Birds: How to Attract Birds to Your Garden.* Emmaus, PA: Rodale, 1996.

Ricciuti, Edward R. *Backyards Are for the Birds: Creating a Bird-Friendly Environment Outside Your Window.* New York: Avon Books, 1998.

Roth, Sally. *Attracting Birds to Your Backyard: 536 Ways to Turn Your Yard and Garden into a Haven for Your Favorite Birds.* Emmaus, PA: Rodale, 1998.

Roth, Sally. *Natural Landscaping.* Emmaus, PA: Rodale, 1997.

Sunset Staff. *An Illustrated Guide to Attracting Birds*. Menlo Park, CA: Sunset Publishing Corporation, 1990.

Terres, John K. *Songbirds in Your Garden*. Chapel Hill, NC: Algonquin Books of Chapel Hill, 1994.

Terres, John K. *The Audubon Society's Encyclopedia of North American Birds*. New York: Random House Value Publishing, 1995.

Thompson III, Bill. *Bird Watching for Dummies*. Foster City, CA: IDG Books Worldwide, Inc., 1997.

Tufts, Craig, and Peter Loewer. *The National Wildlife Federation's Guide to Gardening for Wildlife*. Emmaus, PA.: Rodale, 1995.

For a unique series of books about American birds, chock-full of anecdotes and lively, informative reading, check your local library or secondhand book store for the Life Histories of North American Birds series by Arthur Cleveland Bent, first published in the early decades of the 20th century, and reprinted in paperback by Dover Press. A few titles in the series are:

Life Histories of North American Marsh Birds (1927)

Life Histories of North American Gallinaceous Birds (1980)

Life Histories of North American Flycatchers, Larks, Swallows, and Their Allies (1989)

Life Histories of North American Woodpeckers (1992)

MAGAZINES

Audubon
700 Broadway
New York, NY 10003
Phone: (800) 274-4201
Web site:
    www.audubon.org/index.html

Backyard Bird News
P.O. Box 110
Marietta, OH 45750
Phone: (800) 879-2473
Fax: (740) 373-8443
Web site:
    www.birdwatchersdigest.com

Birder's World
21027 Crossroads Circle
Waukesha, WI 53187-1612
Phone: (800) 533-6644
Web site: www2.birdersworld.com

Birds and Blooms
5400 South 60th Street
Greendale, WI 53129
Phone: (800) 344-6913

Bird Watcher's Digest
P.O. Box 110
Marietta, OH 45750
Phone: (800) 879-2473
Web site:
    www.birdwatchersdigest.com

Living Bird
c/o Cornell Laboratory of
    Ornithology
159 Sapsucker Woods Road
Ithaca, NY 14850
Phone: (800) 843-2473
Web site: www.birds.cornell.edu

Organic Gardening
Rodale Inc.
33 East Minor Street
Emmaus, PA 18098
Phone: (800) 666-2206
    (subscriptions)
Web site:
    www.organicgardening.com

Wild Bird
P.O. Box 52898
Boulder, CO 80322-2898
Phone: (800) 365-4421
Web site: www.animalnetwork.com/
    wildbird

BIRD FIELD GUIDES AND RECORDINGS

The beauty of a field guide lies in its portable nature: These compact books fit easily into a daypack or glove compartment, so you can always have one handy when there's a bird you want to identify. They're also nice to keep near your favorite feeder-watching window so you can look up any unusual guests. Their small size doesn't mean that field guides lack information—on the contrary, they're packed with useful identification tips and may also tell you what foods each bird eats and a little about its nesting habits. Here are a few good ones.

A Guide to Field Identification: Birds of North America, by Chandler S. Robbins, Bertel Bruun, and Herbert S. Zim (New York: Golden Press, 1983). Birds are illustrated in life-like poses and on a plant where you're likely to see them. Range maps are inserted at each bird's entry, so you don't have to flip to a separate section in the back of the book as you do with Peterson's. The book includes all birds of North America, which will give you a wider perspective.

The *Peterson Field Guide* series (Boston: Houghton Mifflin Co., 1998) is also excellent, but the books are regional guides and birds are drawn in flatter, less life-like poses than in the Golden field guide, without any hint of habitat in most pictures. Peterson uses arrows to point out field marks to look for, for definitive identification. Also look for the audio series *Birding by Ear,* which includes *Birding by Ear: Eastern/ Central,* edited by Richard K. Walton (Houghton Mifflin Audio, 1999); it includes three CDs or audiotapes.

The *Audubon Society Field Guide* series (New York: Alfred A. Knopf, 1987), another regional set of guides, uses photos instead of illustrations, which are not as accurate for identifying field marks. The guides also include a lot of interesting information about each bird.

Stokes Field Guide to Birds: Eastern Region and *Stokes Field Guide to Birds: Western Region* (Boston: Little, Brown and Co., 1996) are two photographic field guides that also offer information on feeding and nesting habits and other behavior. There is also a *Stokes Field Guide to Bird Songs: Eastern Region* (or western region) that is by Lang Elliot (Time Warner Audio Books, 1997) and includes three CDs or audiotapes and a booklet.

Index

Note: Page references in **boldface** indicate illustrations.

Ecoregions Map

Plant communities and their associated birds have natural geographical limits, and these limits have been recognized and mapped into a series of areas known as ecoregions. Robert G. Bailey, heading a team of ecologists and geographers, has developed the ecoregions mapping concept. Using climate, topography, and vegetation, Bailey mapped natural boundaries across the continent. This ecoregion system helps the backyard bird watcher better understand seasonal movements and behavior in birds and select plants that will attract birds to the home landscape.

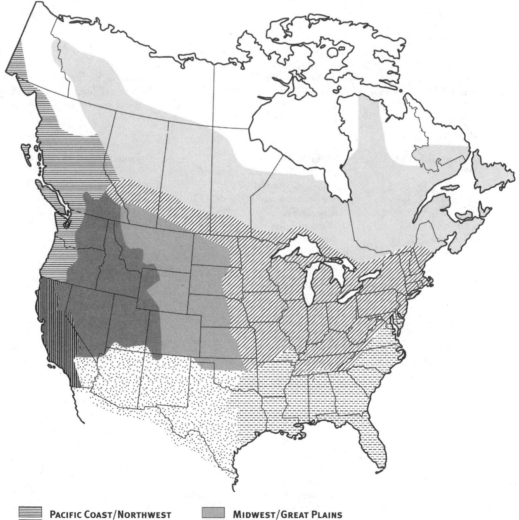

PACIFIC COAST/NORTHWEST
PACIFIC COAST/CALIFORNIA
MOUNTAIN WEST
DESERT SOUTHWEST
MIDWEST/GREAT PLAINS
CONTINENTAL EAST
HUMID SOUTH
CANADIAN NORTH